Sophie...

BEST FRIENDS
ARE FOREVER

TED SLUPIK

FOREWORD BY LAURA T. COFFEY

Sophie...

BEST FRIENDS
ARE FOREVER

For information about this title contact the publisher:

Lizzy Literary Productions LLC
1700 Park Street, #201
Naperville, IL 60563
lizzyliteraryproductionsllc@gmail.com

ISBNs
Hardcover: 978-1-7340784-0-4
Softcover: 978-1-7340784-1-1
eBook: 978-1-7340784-2-8

Printed in the United States of America

Contents

Foreword

THE SPECIAL HEALING POWERS
OF A DOG NAMED SOPHIE

By Laura T. Coffey

Oh, how I wish I could have met Sophie.

But fortunately for me—and for everybody else—Sophie comes to life in the pages of this beautiful book, where she will continue to comfort and heal perceptive humans for many years to come.

Sophie loved to play and have fun, but she also loved to work. The rough-coated collie spent more than a dozen years of her life smiling, listening, and strengthening patients at hospitals and nursing homes in Naperville, Illinois. The role of therapy dogs in hospital settings has been growing fast across the United States; medical professionals can see how much these well-trained dogs reduce stress and cheer people up when they're feeling low. Sophie helped blaze that trail at an unusually young age for a therapy dog, and her legacy and undeniable impact are captured perfectly in *Sophie . . . Best Friends Are Forever.*

As much as this is a book about a remarkable dog with remarkable healing powers, it's also a story about the love and dedication of the dog's handler. I've had the privilege of getting to know author Ted Slupik and his wife, Bernie, and let me tell you something: They are good eggs. Dog lovers everywhere will appreciate the hilariously charming details that emerge in this book and reveal just how much Ted and Bernie adore dogs. They coordinate fun vacation itineraries—for their dogs; they tackle remodeling projects to make home life more enjoyable—for their dogs; they take their furry friends to work and put thought into the timing and variety of special snacks—for their dogs. As you read along and see the Slupiks going to such lengths to keep their dogs happy and comfortable, you're bound to find yourself chuckling and cheering them on.

The Slupiks' big-heartedness and generosity become clear in other ways as well: through their creation of Lizzy's Fund, a philanthropic effort to provide full veterinary, dental, and grooming care for senior dogs in shelter environments and help the dogs find homes; through the thousands of hours of volunteer time Ted and Sophie logged together doing therapy work for people who really needed their visits; and through Ted and Bernie's willingness to learn valuable lessons from dogs, who really do have so much to teach us. Throughout this book, Ted repeatedly reveals just how carefully he was listening whenever Sophie had something important to convey. Beautiful lessons emerge about compassion, contentment, priorities in life—and, most importantly, about love.

Yes, *Sophie . . . Best Friends Are Forever* is a love story—the kind of story anyone who's known the love of a dog will appreciate. It's a joy to become immersed in this story and come to know a dog as special and as unforgettable as Sophie. What a good, good girl.

Laura T. Coffey is the author of the bestselling book My Old Dog: Rescued Pets with Remarkable Second Acts. *She's also a longtime writer, editor, and producer for TODAY.com, the website of NBC's TODAY show. An award-winning journalist with more than two decades of experience, Laura has written and edited hundreds of high-profile human-interest stories. She lives in Seattle, Washington. Her website is www. MyOldDogBook.com.*

Preface

This is the story of Sophie, a rough-coated collie, who came into my life in November 2001. She was born September 10, 2001, the day before the infamous September 11th. She passed away June 17, 2015, after almost fourteen years of a remarkable life. Here is a picture of Sophie at ten weeks of age.

Sophie spent almost thirteen years doing therapy work at hospitals and nursing homes. We were a team. She touched and helped more lives than I could count or remember. Sophie was not my first, nor my last dog, but she was the most special dog I have ever known. Typical collie qualities are loyalty, humor, obedience and devotion to their owner. Sophie appeared to have them all. Sophie was born to make other people happy and feel better about themselves; something she practiced every day.

Sophie and her Nana, an Alzheimer's patient

In addition to the above, Sophie could be a quiet companion, providing comfort and guidance. Sophie possessed qualities that all people should have: compassion, kindness, humility, gentleness, and patience. She also had an unquestioning devotion and obedience to the people around her, even if she had just met them.

She made people who were sad feel better. I believe she certainly had an emotional healing power and, in some instances, even a physical healing power.

Given her unusual size (too long for the collie standard), Sophie was a breeder's reject who proved that where you come from doesn't matter. What you do with your life is what counts. Sophie would sit next to people, look at their face and expressions and listen to them. It was as if she understood every word they said. I wonder if she knew and understood more than any of us realized.

Sophie was a very gentle dog who had a sense of balance in her life between work and play to a degree which is lacking in most people I know. She was not a one-person dog; she was a family dog. Everyone in her inner circle of family and friends benefited from her temperament and character. Sophie had a very sweet disposition, and she loved the chance to be the center of attention. Her coloring was the epitome of the collie breed standard with beautiful reddish shades in her fur, from the lightest buff to the deepest chestnut.

For several weeks after Sophie passed, I started remembering things about her life. She made a difference in people's lives that she touched, both in her therapy work and in everyday life, so I started to write a brief description of them down. I began with two or three phrases of each event so I would remember how much she impacted so many people's lives, made things better, changed someone's life, or made them happy.

The term "therapy dog" refers to a dog trained to provide affection and comfort to people in hospitals, retirement homes, nursing homes, schools, and stressful situations, such as disaster areas.

The concept of a therapy dog is often attributed to Elaine Smith, an American who worked as a registered nurse for a time in England. Smith noticed how well patients responded to visits by a certain chaplain and his canine companion.

Many health care providers now recognize the therapeutic effect of animal companionship, such as relieving stress, lowering blood pressure, and raising spirits, and the demand for therapy dogs continues to grow.

Today the three largest associations of therapy dogs are:

Alliance of Therapy Dogs	15,000 teams
Pet Partners	16,000 teams
Therapy Dogs International	12,000 teams

The AKC (American Kennel Club) has recently recognized the importance and value of therapy dogs and allows dogs to qualify for certain distinctions. An AKC Therapy Dog Distinguished (THDD) must have completed four hundred visits. Had it been available at the time of her service, Sophie would have easily exceeded the number of visits required for this recognition.

Animal Assisted Therapy (AAT) utilizes the human-animal bond to bring comfort to patients and serve as a diversion from their illness. Visits by therapy dogs can help in the healing process. All of this has become very well documented. Sophie became certified as a therapy dog at the age of one, the earliest age that a dog is allowed to qualify. We were required to complete an intensive four-day training program to obtain our certification.

Sophie and I worked together for almost thirteen years of certified therapy work. Even though it was physically difficult for her at the end, she still had a positive effect on someone almost every time she visited a hospital, nursing home, or any group of people. Over her lifetime, she met well over five thousand patients and visitors. Near the end of her work, she attained celebrity status at the facilities she visited, as almost all of the staff knew her.

After writing down hundreds of different things Sophie did over her lifetime, I started realizing what had happened in Sophie's contacts with others which I originally thought was coincidence, was not. If you were to ask yourself "What was most important in your life and where did you make a differ-ence?" most of us would be hard pressed to come up with a list of ten items. When I had accumulated hundreds of "Sophie" stories, I finally realized the special purpose and impact of Sophie's almost fourteen-year life, and I wanted to share those wonderful stories.

Most of us do not recognize the best times of our lives until they have passed. I now realize all those trips with Sophie to the hospital or nursing home, where we met people to make them feel better or less lonely, were the best times of my life. Sophie certainly was obedient and attentive. The gentleness in her nature was part of her spirit. Once she got into a patient's room, what she learned from me was not important, it was her instincts. It was all Sophie. The interreactions she had with thousands of people were her skills and special healing power. I just happened to be lucky enough to witness it.

I wrote this book to honor Sophie's memory and to make people realize how important it is to give back in this world. The more you give, the more good comes to you. With Sophie, every day was a new beginning: starting with a clean slate. She always left the patients and visitors that she interreacted with happy, and created a state of emotional healing.

Sophie showed me that every day is a gift.

Introduction

It had been a busy and long week at work, and I stayed late until almost 7:00 p.m., Monday through Thursday. Now it is 4:00 p.m. on Friday and I am rushing home from work. I need to get home to change clothes, feed and walk Sophie, and be at the hospital by 6:00 p.m. I'm tired, and the last thing I feel like doing is spending three hours in a warm hospital trying to visit what always seemed like an endless list of patients. As soon as I turn on to my street, however, I see Sophie's happy face in my front family room window and my weariness dissipates. We have a job to do, and participating in the hospital's Animal Assisted Therapy (AAT) program is an important one. Starting with fifteen dogs, the program has now grown to over eighty.

As I enter my house, Sophie's infectious joy takes over. She is "on." I left my blue volunteer jacket hanging on the back of the kitchen chair before I left for work this morning, and Sophie has had the whole day to anticipate tonight's activities as part of her therapy dog job at the hospital. With that jacket and both of our I.D. tags, we could go almost anywhere in the hospital. This job makes her happy, and her happiness transcends to everyone she comes into contact with.

A well-worn twelve-year-old jacket

People might find it difficult to believe Sophie knew it was her work day just from seeing my volunteer jacket, but I have no doubt that she did. The joy she felt every other Friday night for over twelve years created an enormous amount of beautiful memories which I will cherish forever.

This is the special story of Sophie . . . her remarkable life, the lives she touched, and the lessons we both learned.

CHAPTER 1

Sophie and the Middle Years

By the time Sophie was the age of three, she knew the routine of visiting patients and following the required rules of the hospital. She performed her job perfectly. Sophie knew all the manners of going in and out of a patient's room and introducing herself to them, their visitors, plus any doctors and nurses present. But the interreaction with the patients, staff, and visitors was all Sophie. She had the talent of making a first impression on people as if they had known her all her life. Sophie went up to whomever you introduced her to, and looked at or nudged the person until she obtained a reaction. She was very kind, gentle, open and interested in whatever the patient, visitor or staff had to say. Sophie would look you in the eye, tip her head from side to side, and respond to your voice and mannerisms. She would react differently, depending on what people she met in the room. She knew the difference between sick and well, young and old, and how to make the patient the most important person in the room.

The more attention you gave Sophie, the more attention she *wanted* to give you. She wanted to visit everyone she greeted, but if she felt the person's emotions and acceptance toward her, she wanted to stay even longer with that person. We would walk into a room at the hospital on a Friday night, and a lot of visitors were always present. After her introduction to the patient, she always made sure to introduce herself, one by one, to everyone else in the room.

Over the years, we visited many special friends and family at the hospital. Even if it was not our scheduled workday, we were allowed to visit patients we knew as long as we wore our tags and uniform. Sophie was able to visit my father-in-law, my mother-in-law, my mother, and other friends of the family who knew Sophie well. Whenever a friend or a family member was in the hospital, Sophie was available by appointment only. Many

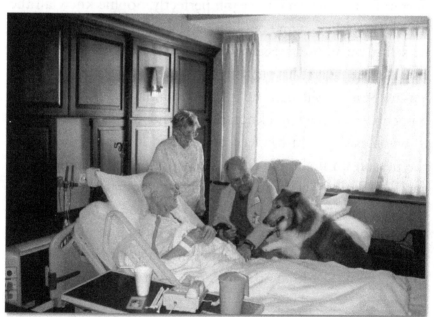

Sophie visiting Grandpa and Nana

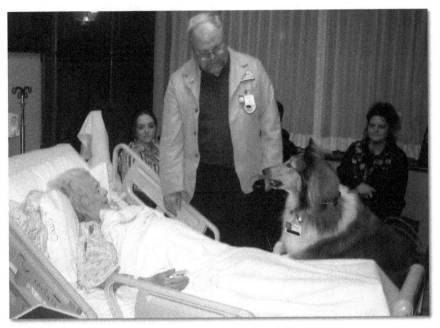

Sophie visiting her Grandma

of them were astonished to see her, as they were not sure what she did at the hospital. They knew she had a job there, but weren't quite certain of what therapy work was. Of course, Sophie always recognized family and friends and put out the extra effort to make them feel better.

Most volunteers did not want to give up their Friday nights from 6:00–9:00 p.m., so there were three or four handlers who became regulars. The four of us handlers got to be good friends and looked out for each other and our dogs on Friday nights. As a group, we would come together in the volunteer room to start the night, call to alert the nurses by floor as to whom was visiting, and leave together to do our rounds. This gave the nurses a bit of time to recheck if any other patients wanted to see a dog. If one person had more patients to see on a floor and the rest of us were done with our floor, we would go and help out the remaining person until every patient who wanted a visit on that unit had received a visit.

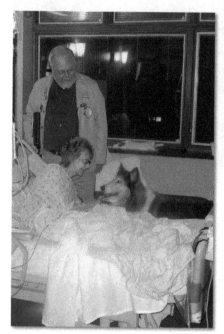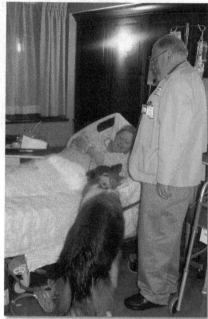

Sophie visiting new friends

Sophie visited many of our friends, which often had a remarkable effect on both of us. One was a man named Ken in his seventies, a neighbor of mine who had fought prostate cancer for over twenty years. Cancer was finally getting the best of him. As we walked in the room to see him, Ken was on a phone call. He motioned for us to come in. Sitting and waiting for him to finish his call, we could hear he was making arrangements to donate his car to a local charity. Ken knew he was going to die soon.

On the phone, Ken explained that he wanted to know his car would be picked up within the next few days. (As it turned out, his car went to someone who was down on their luck and needed a car to get to and from work.) How much of an example could one man be? Ken was nearing death, but making an effort to help someone else before he passed.

Recognizing Ken, Sophie sat intently watching and listening to him on the phone. Our usual encounter was to see Ken gardening in his yard. Sophie knew this was different, as this strong and vibrant man was weak and in bed. We saw him two or three times before he died, and Sophie understood what was going on. She showed extra love and attention to thank him for his friendship over the years. Sophie instinctively knew he was not going to live, but if you talked to him, you would never know it was coming. Ken was upbeat until the end of his life. What a lesson for all of us to learn. Ken would look at Sophie, telling her she was a "good girl" and thanking her for coming. Sophie made eye contact with Ken, expressing kindness, gentleness, and peace. The last time we saw Ken, he said his goodbyes, and Sophie and I walked away very sad.

On each hospital floor, there was a large sitting room with a couch and some chairs. The room wall exterior and door were clear glass so you could see both in and out. Sometimes a patient was in that room meeting with family or with a doctor. Other times it was a family waiting for a patient to come back from surgery or tests, and sometimes it was occupied by a grieving family. Whenever Sophie saw people in that sitting room, she knew everyone in there probably needed some extra help and attention. If I did not notice anyone in the room, Sophie would notice and instinctively pull me into the room until she had a chance to comfort and visit with all the rooms' inhabitants. Of course, she became the center of attention for everyone in the room, and many times an emotional outlet for people who needed comfort or just wanted to hug a dog.

The hospital group also had several social activities during the year for the volunteers at the hospital for the Animal Assisted Therapy (AAT) group. During one of the events, members brought their dogs along with them. At a therapy dog picnic, just as she was at her first training session, Sophie was most interested in meeting the people and all the handlers that attended. She did not show much of an interest in the dogs, only their owners. I would take her around to meet everyone, and she remembered and recognized who we had worked with. She waited patiently to be acknowledged and petted, then moved on to the next person.

Another activity we participated in the first year we were in the program was the annual Halloween parade through the hospital. The dogs dressed up and marched and quickly went in and out of rooms on every floor. We traveled through the rooms in a long line. No visits were done at the hospital that day, and it was an opportunity to create awareness of the program. The patients and staff either thought it was cute or laughed at the dogs. I had bought a child's costume of a ladybug for Sophie. Sophie looked and felt silly, but I left it on. Sophie did not enjoy being dressed up, and I never did this to her again.

Miss Ladybug on Halloween

Over the years, we had many special requests from patients at the hospital. Visitors would see us walk in on the main floor and come up to us and say, "Please be sure to go see my mom or dad or friend in such and such room." Our team would discuss with the patients what other dogs were on the shift that day. If there was a request for a special breed of dog (collie), we made sure that person got a second visit from the dog they would like to see. We were the only collie in the program, and many of the senior citizens on the orthopedic floor were very fond of collies. Sophie received many special requests. Patients called from their rooms to request a visit when they saw us walking down the hallways.

Sophie's team therapy dog cards

In the early years, three of Sophie's friends on Friday nights were Molly, a golden retriever, Little Pretty, a long-haired dachshund, and Cherry, a Scottish terrier. These dogs were almost as good as Sophie in mannerisms and temperament, but still not as good as her. I believe that the eight of us were the best team in the hospital. Patients looked forward to seeing us.

Many nurses would share with us the reactions and comments patients made after having a dog visit. The dogs became good friends with some of the regular staff, and Sophie was recognized by many nurses and doctors.

Dr. Mark, one of the top cardiologists at the hospital, who recognized and remembered Sophie from a few years prior, called out to her by name and she responded. I asked Dr. Mark how he could remember Sophie from one encounter several years prior, as he had to have several thousand patients. He remarked that he had over six thousand patients. Sophie must have made a remarkable impression in a three-minute visit for this doctor to remember her by name.

The job of being a therapy dog at the hospital was not easy; it was a high stress job. Dogs had to have the ability to concentrate and were tired at the end of their shift.

1. The dog was required to be under the handler's control at all times.

2. Control began and ended at the car door.

3. No dog-to-dog interaction on a hospital floor or in a patient room was allowed.

4. At the nurses' station, the handler placed the dog in a sit/ stay to respect staff that may be afraid of dogs or did not wish to have contact.

The rules discussed were only a small part of the policies developed. All were meant to keep the dogs and patients safe. The rules required the dog to heel at the handler's side while walking through the hallways, heel into and out of rooms; and get into a sit position and request permission of the patient before entering the room. Even though we had a list of the patients who wanted to see us, sometimes there was a mix-up and they did not want to see us after all. In some cases, the patient was not feeling well at the time and had changed their mind. More often than that, somebody wanted to see us and did not make the list we were originally given by the staff. In that case, the rules required that we not enter the room but first contact the charge nurse of that patient to get her permission to add the patient to the therapy dog visit list.

On one occasion, we entered a room with an elderly female patient, and a few minutes later two nurses came in and insisted that we had to leave immediately. As it turns out, this patient, named Phyllis, had been quarantined with an infectious disease. The sign on the outside of the door had fallen down, and we had no idea we should not have entered the room. We had spent almost five minutes in the room conversing with Phyllis before the nurses came to get us. Phyllis was an elderly lady who loved Sophie and enjoyed my contact with her as well, and she had shaken hands with me. As it turned out, Phyllis had been in isolation for over a week, without seeing any friends or family. No wonder she was most anxious to reach out to anyone who would speak to her after this period of solitary confinement.

After leaving the room, I asked the nurses what I should do and what was the problem with the patient in the room. Based on hospital and HIPPA (privacy) rules, the nurses would not tell me what was wrong with the patient. They told me to go home immediately and bathe the dog. When I asked them what I should do, they suggested I go home, take my clothes off in the garage, put them in a bag, and throw them in the garbage. This sounded quite serious, and they would still not tell me what was going on or give me any details. Sophie and I were escorted out of the hospital to be sure that we left. She looked at the security person almost asking, "What did we do? We haven't done anything wrong."

Sophie and I went home and did what we were told. However, my wife was quite concerned and called back to the hospital to find out further information. She asked if they could ask Phyllis for her permission to reveal what her diagnosis was. The nurse replied and said she couldn't because the woman had dementia. My wife then asked if the nurses could ask some of her family for permission to disclose her illness, and the woman had no family. Finally going up the chain of command ladder at the hospital, and after an hour of phone calls, my wife talked to the head charge nurse of the entire hospital, who gave her the diagnosis. It was an infectious disease, but neither Sophie nor I were ever affected by it. If nothing else, it made us double-check entry to a room from then on, even if that patient was on the list for a visit. At the entry to every room, I taught Sophie to stop, wait, and look. We never missed a sign again. She obviously couldn't read, but her remembering to stop automatically at the entrance to the room reminded me to do the double-check before entering.

Sophie had a wonderful sense of knowing the patient she was visiting with. Her mannerisms would be different around old versus young people, around children versus adults. In instances where she came across either a physically handicapped child or an autistic child, her behavior became even gentler and kinder for that child. Sophie seemed to have a sixth sense.

If the patient happened to be busy when we came to their room, they would often ask if we could come back later. Sometimes they would ask if we could come back when their family was visiting later that night. We always tried to honor the request, so Friday night therapy for Sophie and me often became longer nights than scheduled. We tried to make the extra effort each Friday: Sophie could not resist greeting someone new, even after two or three hours of work.

There were occasions when people or patients were having a bad day and did not want to see us. Sophie and I learned to accept it; rejection never seemed to get her down. If we were not allowed to enter, her ears would go back and she would slowly walk away. She knew we couldn't enter the room and went on to the next room to start all over again. Sophie did a lot better in accepting the circumstances than I did. She never dwelled on the rejection. Sophie had a bounce-back personality, and kept doing her job the best she could, starting with the next patient. You could tell from her mannerisms and response to the next patient, Sophie viewed every visit like the first visit of the night.

Since we were at the hospital for several hours, we would take a "coffee break" about two-thirds of the way through the night. I would go to the employee break room with Sophie and fill a large Styrofoam cup with ice and water. I would have the first two sips, and Sophie would have whatever was left if she wanted it. She didn't like drinking out of that type of cup. Come to think about it, neither did I.

At about six months of age, I taught Sophie hand signals, as soon as she had learned the verbal commands. With the verbal command, I would teach Sophie what I wanted her to do, and then simultaneously apply the hand signal to it. I then gradually removed the verbal command until Sophie responded to the hand signal only. I had never really read any books on hand signals, and most of the hand signals I made up were different from what I later learned were the standard signals from the dog training books I read. So it was our special language that no one else knew, even if you were familiar with training dogs. Some of the signals were very slight, and unless you were looking for them, you would never notice them. This created an opportunity for Sophie to amaze many patients.

One of the commands she knew was to "watch me." Sophie was asked to sit, stay, and watch wherever I went. The signal for "watch me" was for me to touch my nose. I then moved about the room. Sophie would sit and stay, and then watch me with her big brown eyes wherever I went in the room. She would not take her eyes off me. Sometimes I used this activity to cheer up some of the patients. I would go into the corner of the hall just outside of the room, or stand behind some visitors, and Sophie would strain her neck to keep her eye on me, but never leave her stay command. The patients would get a kick out of Sophie straining to watch me wherever she was in the room. She would not move until I came back to her and released her by touching her nose with my finger and then touching my nose.

Sophie remembered most of the hand signals I taught her until her last visit. Her hearing during the last several years of her life showed a small loss, so working with hand signals helped us stay within the hospital routine. Most of the time Sophie was acting on her own, but on occasion a little hand signal helped.

One of the other items I taught her was to say good night to the patients with a short speak. I would just ask her to say good night, and through sleight-of-hand give her the signal to say good night. I even had patients ask her to say good night to them. And she would on my command, but it came across as if she was responding directly to their request.

One of the other things the hospital program did was to develop a picture card of the dogs to leave behind for the patient to remember the dog's visit. The front of the card was a picture of the dog, and on the back was her date of birth and some facts about the dog. People who were in the hospital before or just families with the patients or visitors, used to come up to us and ask us for a card because Sophie was so beautiful. The amazing thing about the card was that the picture was taken of Sophie at one year old.

Sophie

Breed: Rough Collie
DOB: 9/10/01
Weight: 70 Pounds
Owner/Guardian: Ted

Breed Characteristics:

This "Lassie" dog's heritage is from Scotland, where these highly intelligent herding dogs are known for their tireless work ethic, not to mention their loyalty. They are rugged yet gentle, graceful yet strong.

Sophie came to her owner from the Lamb's Farm. She immediately impressed her new family with her intelligence and lovingness. She has been to obedience classes where her performance was amazing. At home, Sophie enjoys the outdoors – long walks, carrying sticks she finds, and chasing balls. Always having been a "people person," she seems to take great pleasure in meeting new people which makes her assignment of making friends of patients, visitors, and staff at Edward Hospital such a perfect fit for her.

Official hospital I.D. card

Remarkably, Sophie looked the same until her last year in the hospital. No one could believe she was a ten- or twelve-year-old dog when compared to her one-year-old picture. Sophie still worked with her usual mannerisms and enthusiasm while visiting. As hard as it was at the end of her career for Sophie to visit, there was not a time that she did not make a difference with at least one or two people during a night of visiting. Neither Sophie nor I wanted to give up that experience, and I think that's what kept her going to the very end. She couldn't visit the whole hospital on her own anymore, nor could she work three and a half hours, but she still wanted to go for two hours, even though I could see her hips and her arthritis started to bother her. With her adrenalin flowing, we both seemed to be able to forget about any aches, pains or tiredness we had and concentrated on making people happy. When Sophie laid down in a patient's room, I knew it was time to go.

Sophie's whole being and purpose in life was to make others feel better. There are a few people here on Earth who can say they devoted their whole life to making things better. In a special way, even though a dog, Sophie made things better every Friday night for a whole lot of people. I was constantly enriched seeing the people's reaction to her attention and affection. I didn't realize it was one of the best things in my life until it was over. I knew it was special, but finally realized just how special it became for the people who Sophie touched.

Now I want to let you in on how it all began: the occurrence of an amazing series of facts and circumstances aligning themselves to create the story of Sophie.

Sophie, relaxing after work

CHAPTER 2

Finding Sophie

Sophie was our third family dog. Our first dog came about in an unusual way. My children were young (nine and seven) and were interested in getting a dog. My mother (their Grandmother) was staying with us and encouraged my seven-year-old daughter to start asking for a dog every day. She would repeatedly ask, "When can we get a dog?" When that strategy did not seem to be working, her Grandmother told my daughter to start writing notes and leaving them for me. I found notes on my chair; I found notes in my socks; I found notes in my briefcase. In other words, I found notes wherever I looked.

Finally, I decided to find out what was out there in the way of dogs we could adopt. Not doing much thinking about the process nor thinking of the consequences, I called the local pound in town and asked if they had any dogs. This was on a Saturday afternoon and they said they did have a few dogs, so I took a trip to the pound by myself. I was totally unprepared. I had nothing to use to take a dog home; no crate in the car, no leash, no towel, no food, nothing.

Brownie, our first rescue

I walked into the county pound and asked if they had any younger dogs. They brought me to a fenced-in cement area where a brown-and-white mixed-breed puppy was shaking and hiding in the corner. The supervisor indicated the dog was about twelve weeks old. She had been found in a low branch of a hanging tree with a collar. It had been four days and no one had claimed the dog. At that point in time, dogs were not held for a very long period of time in the pound, and if this dog was not adopted, she would be put down at the end of the day. That was good enough for me. I made the decision, and of course I took her.

Since I was by myself and had no means to transport her, I carried her to the car and put her on my lap. As I started to drive home, I called my wife and asked her to meet me partway from home. I had a doctor appointment, and she needed to take the dog home. The dog spent the entire time on my lap shivering and shaking and looking at me. I looked at her sad face and big brown eyes and came up with her name: Brownie. I later learned from the vet that she was a mix of a beagle and Jack Russell terrier, approximately twelve weeks old.

The family loved her immediately. Brownie was a very loyal and energetic dog. She was protective of the family, and when anyone else came to the house she barked at them suspiciously. If anyone in the family was sick, Brownie would sit or sleep next to that person until she could sense that person was well.

Brownie's training was unorthodox. My wife would walk Brownie up and down the block and have her sit, heel, or stay. I walked behind them, and if Brownie did not react properly, I dropped a small bean bag on Brownie. It did not hurt her, but it was like a lightning bolt coming out of nowhere from above. Brownie learned her manners quickly.

One of Brownie's favorite activities happened at dinnertime. She would come to the counter where her food was stored and sit next to it. When her bowl was pulled out, she would jump up and down to the height of the counter of twenty-nine inches to see her food. This small, twelve-pound dog was able to do a vertical jump up and down wherein her head was above the countertop from a standstill. Although this appeared very cute, over time I think this had a negative effect on her back in later life.

Brownie developed back problems at the age of seven and had a herniated disc. We chose to treat her with the most conservative treatment for her, which was to let her rest and give her some muscle relaxants and steroids. After a period of three to four weeks, she seemed to recover. From that point on, I took her on long, multiple walks a day to strengthen her back muscles. But she had these instances the rest of her life, and it would contribute to her being put down at close to the age of thirteen.

On Valentine's Day in 1993, when Brownie was eight years old, my wife was with a client doing some accounting work. This client had a Chihuahua at their home office whose name was Jalapeno. Jalapeno was a chunky dog who had a favorite activity of riding on a vacuum cleaner as the room was being vacuumed. This dog created a bond with my wife every time she came out to visit to do the monthly update of the books.

On February 14, 1993, the client walked into the office with a little red collar and said, "Surprise, Happy Valentine's Day!" That was the beginning

Lizzy at eight weeks old, sleeping in a slipper

of Lizzy. We later learned she was a very small Chihuahua that was taken from her mother by a breeder at five weeks of age.

This is almost the worst thing you can do for a puppy, as it does not allow the mother enough time to teach her litter anything. We did not know about any of this at the time. When my wife called me from the client's office and asked, "What do I do about this dog?" I responded, "Leave it with our client!" Of course, my wife decided to bring the dog home anyway. Lizzy weighed less than a pound when my wife brought her home. She came home and slept in a house slipper.

Again, we were not prepared in any way for another dog.

In the beginning Lizzy was afraid and timid, probably because of the removal from her mother at such a young age. After the dog came to our house, we kept her in a crate to train her. She was too small for a dog crate, so we bought a hamster crate for her to sleep in and to be trained.

Lizzy and Brownie

The first several weeks of having Lizzy, I strongly resisted having another dog. But over time I began to accept her. She seemed so vulnerable. Chihuahuas are different from most dogs in that they turn into a one-person dog. Even though my wife provided most of the hands-on care with Lizzy, including feeding and crate training and taking her out, Lizzy became attached to me. She learned to wait at the front door for me, sit in the chair every night reading with me, and come up to the chair and bark for my immediate attention. I became very attached to little Lizzy. Lizzy was a real lapdog, enjoyed affection, petting, and cuddling. She was not a dog who could do a lot of tricks or a lot of special things, which I also attributed to her leaving her mother at such a young age.

Lizzy spent six years growing up with Brownie until Brownie passed away. Over time, she did learn a few simple dog tricks, probably from watching Brownie. Her favorite trick was to roll over. She would do it multiple times, part for the attention and, of course, for a cookie. Near the end of her life, she perfected her trick and once rolled over twelve consecutive times. I am sure Lizzy thought Brownie was her mother, as she followed her everywhere. The two became very good companions; going

Lizzy watching baseball at age eleven

on walks together, lying together, and even sleeping next to each other as close as possible.

Lizzy's favorite activity was sitting on the couch watching baseball on television. We never figured out why she liked baseball. At first we thought it had something to do the green screen. But she had no interest in football, golf, or anything else on television with the green screen, except baseball. In later years when a commercial came on, Lizzy would doze off until the baseball broadcast resumed. Then she perked back up. She would be able to sit for hours at a time watching a baseball game. Some people believe in reincarnation and the fact that we come back as a different type of being. If that is true, Lizzy must have been a baseball player in a previous life.

In January 1998, Brownie experienced another back disc injury and was put on steroids again. She probably was left too long on the drug and would get hyper in the crate where we were keeping her to calm her down. As a result, she had a stroke. We took her to the emergency vet, and as we were leaving, Lizzy cried out to Brownie. Dogs must know more than we think. And they certainly know how to communicate with each other. By the time we got to the emergency vet on that Sunday night, we understood we would most likely have to put Brownie down. She had a very slight chance of recovery, and her big brown eyes showed that she was ready to give up. She had suffered quite a bit, and we didn't want to prolong her suffering.

Afterward, we came home and sat with Lizzy for the rest of the night and wondered how she would experience her loss. Lizzy spent many days and weeks looking for her friend Brownie. She became very restless at night and did not sleep. She still slept downstairs in the family room, which is where she used to sleep with Brownie, but now she was by herself. In talking to the owner of one of the local pet stores, he suggested we put Lizzy's bed in the place Brownie used to sleep. That worked. Lizzy then settled down and adjusted to her life as an only dog, which is how it would be for the next three years.

After those three years, Lizzy was now nine and we started to think about getting another dog. Even though Lizzy was a Chihuahua, and small dogs tend to live a long time, we had not really thought of how long she might live. It would turn out that she lived a lot longer than we ever imagined.

Our quest for another dog started in 2000. We went to various pet stores and looked at many breeds, including labs, beagles, and other bigger dogs. We had to find a dog that would be compatible with a five-pound, nine-year-old Chihuahua. This turned out to be a difficult task. Whenever the pet store or breeder brought the potential sibling to the playroom where we had Lizzy, all the puppies seem to go after Lizzy and almost maul her. She was somewhat frail, and none of the dogs seemed to work.

Then I had the idea of getting a collie, as they seemed to be gentler, larger dogs. I don't know if it was because I grew up with the *Lassie* television show, but I had always wanted a collie. My wife was not too certain about getting another dog, as our children were grown and were now out of college and the house. We looked at several collie breeders and were disappointed. At the time, collies were not very popular amongst breeders and there weren't many to pick from. One of the breeders we went to had over twenty dogs, and her kennels were in a residential neighborhood. Due to neighbor complaints, she had de-barked almost all of her adult dogs that she was breeding. It was the most pitiful sound you can imagine, a collie trying to express itself, straining to be heard, and having no bark. It seemed so cruel. Collies have such a wonderful bark. That was enough for us to not even consider adopting a dog from that breeder.

We looked at another one or two collie breeders, including one who had border collies as well, but we just didn't find a fit. After about a year of unsuccessful looking, we decided to give up and accept that Lizzy would be our only dog.

In November 2001, a series of incredible coincidences (I think not) would allow us to find Sophie and make her part of our life. The world was turned upside down on Sept. 11, 2001, with the terrorism tragedy on the East Coast. Sophie was born late in the day on Sept. 10, 2001. We were friends with a couple in our neighborhood that belonged to the same church. They had two children the same ages as ours and were in the same grade, middle, and high schools together. We had known them for a long time, and we thought we knew them well. We saw them often at church and school activities, and they seemed to have a perfectly normal life. Both were working, had great jobs, their house was immaculate, their yard was perfect. We thought that they were the perfect family.

Our lives were turned upside down in early November of 2001 when our doorbell rang. It was our friend (the wife), terrified, asking for help. She was very disturbed, and her hair and clothes were disheveled. We took her into our house, and she immediately began to tell us the horrible story of what happened to her over the years. She had become a victim of physical abuse. We had to get her some protection. Although there were many women's shelters in Naperville, they were all full that day. She could not go back to her house, as it put her in danger. We called her children, who were away at school, and told them what had happened.

After a long discussion with their oldest daughter, we decided it was appropriate to call the police. Within ten minutes, we had many police cars storming down the street as if they were about to raid our house. It certainly attracted a lot of attention from the neighbors. The police interviewed our friend and decided they were going to go back to her house and arrest her husband for physical abuse of his spouse, our friend. The police proceeded to arrest him, and while he was in custody, he took his own life. What a horrible end to a family life that no one would have ever suspected had anything wrong. After several days, our friend left our house and stayed with her family in another state.

My wife and I were stunned and replayed the event over and over again with its depressing outcome. We decided to try to cheer ourselves up. My wife suggested we go look for a dog, which I was very surprised at. We went to the local pet store, as obviously we still hadn't learned our lesson, and found nothing. This was on a Sunday. Now our interest in finding another dog was rekindled.

The following Friday I went to a client up north in Lake Bluff and finished work early, leaving at three o'clock. On the way home, I drove past Lambs Farm. Lambs Farm had a pet store run by individuals with developmental disabilities. They received dogs that were not considered to be a breed standard as donations from breeders. These dogs were then sold to raise money for Lambs Farm and the program. Just by chance, I pulled into the parking lot at 3:45 p.m., noting that the pet shop closed at four o'clock, only fifteen minutes away. The lights were dim, but the employees inside let me look for five minutes before they closed the doors. Another coincidence? I think not. As soon as I walked in, I spotted an area in the back with a larger pen that had two collies approximately eight weeks old. They were a male and a female, a brother and a sister, and the sister turned out to be Sophie. Even if I had wanted to take her that day, there was not enough time to process the paperwork. I didn't really want to do that without seeing how she would react with Lizzy and how my wife would be with the choice.

I anxiously waited till Saturday morning to see if this would work. Lambs Farm opened on Saturday morning at ten o'clock. On that Friday afternoon, the employee said to get there early, and then we could come and pick up the dog. As it turned out, we were there shortly before ten o'clock. Unfortunately, there was a line of eight or nine other people in front of us. I thought to myself, *This quest of all these years will come so close, and someone will adopt the collies before it's our turn.*

Most of the people in line were looking at smaller dogs and had no interest in bigger dogs. Our number was called and the two collies were still available! They brought Sophie into the playroom, and we noticed immediately how gentle she was as a puppy. Sophie was very alert and attentive and very interested in us.

The final test was about to begin. We had brought Lizzy in the car with us. I brought Lizzy into the playroom with Sophie to see what Sophie's reaction would be. (Now, remember, you had an almost nine-year old, five-pound Chihuahua with a ten-pound, eight-week-old collie puppy.) Sophie the puppy went down on all fours and was very submissive to Lizzy. Lizzy walked around her and sniffed her while Sophie was still lying in a down position. Sophie did not get up, bark, or jump on Lizzy, or show any sort of aggressive behavior. Unbelievable as it seemed, we had finally found the perfect match. We brought Sophie to her forever home that afternoon.

This time we were much more prepared for our first collie. We had purchased a giant crate to transport her home. When we got home, we set up the crate with some blankets inside, including one of Lizzy's. Our first day in training was about to begin a long journey. We still had no idea of Sophie's personality, other than she was very gentle and not rambunctious with the Chihuahua. We would find out she was much more than that in the weeks to come. Later that month, we would host Thanksgiving for our family, which was about forty people at our house at one time. We'd have to start training quickly in prepare Sophie to meet the rest of her family.

Sophie, age one, and Lizzy, age nine

CHAPTER 3

Teach Me All You Can

It didn't take long to come up with the name for Sophie. Although we had a few other names in mind, including Sophia, we quickly settled on Sophie, as it matched her personality of a simple, happy dog. She spent the first afternoon and night with us playing and sleeping. We put Sophie in the crate at night downstairs next to Lizzy's bed and got up early the next morning to check on her. She was very quiet during the night and did not cry.

Dogs do not like to mess in their crate. Sophie had her first and only accident the first night, and it was a strong incentive for her to become potty trained. She did not have any other accidents until she was much older (twelve or thirteen), and ill. I found it amusing that you could potty train a dog in one night, whereas a child requires a much longer period of time. If we could only translate that knowledge to children, raising babies would be a whole lot easier.

We called our friends, Linda and Larry, and invited them over to see our new dog, Sophie. During the first couple of days, we

At eight weeks old, having a nap

called her "Little Sophie," as we sometimes called the Chihuahua "Little Lizzy." When our friends came over and were introduced to "Little Sophie," they noted how big Sophie's feet already were. They said, "This dog is not going to be a little collie based on the size of her feet." They turned out to be right after all. Most female collies grow up to be in the fifty-five- to sixty-pound range. Sophie at her prime would weigh up to seventy pounds. She was the size of a male collie in a female's body. She had the four white paws, a white breast, and beautiful chestnut/mahogany coloring over the rest of her body. She was what is considered a sable white with mahogany markings. Her markings and coloring were perfect and true to her breed. I cannot tell you the hundreds of times people would say, "What a beautiful dog!"

One of the most important things we wanted to teach Sophie in the beginning was respect for Lizzy and the boundaries of where she was permitted in the house. Based on her initial encounter and submissive behavior toward Lizzy, from day one it was obvious that Lizzy was the boss. Lizzy maintained her status as the boss (the alpha dog) until she passed away at almost sixteen and a half years when Sophie was seven. They spent many wonderful years together. Sophie was a quick learner of the house boundaries as well, primarily learning from watching Lizzy's behavior. In the beginning we wanted to restrict Sophie's place to be in the laundry room and the family room. We did not permit her in the kitchen, leaving that as a safe haven for Lizzy, if needed. The living room and dining rooms were also off-limits to both Lizzy and Sophie, as were all of the upstairs rooms to both dogs. We taught Sophie the boundaries with the simple command of "no." We did not need to use gates or other restraints as part of the training.

We continued to feed Lizzy by herself in the kitchen and Sophie in the laundry room for the first month they lived together. We wanted no conflict between the two dogs over food, especially due to their size difference. After an amazingly short period of time (a month), we began to let the two dogs eat together in the laundry room. There were no problems, and Sophie never tried to eat any of Lizzy's food. Lizzy was permitted to take from Sophie's bowl, but not vice versa. Sophie would always share her food with another dog or person. She was not territorial at all and would often bring you her bone to share as well.

On the third day in our home, and for some unknown reason, Sophie had a seizure. She lay on the floor for ten to fifteen seconds and lost control of her muscles and nerves. We called our friend and pet sitter, who told us the best thing to do would be to take Sophie back to Lambs Farm, as there was some obvious physical problem that we did not want to deal with. We also called our vet, who had the same opinion. My wife was concerned as well, but my gut feeling said that Sophie would be all right, even though the pet sitter and the vet wanted us to take Sophie back. I stood my ground to give Sophie another chance.

I learned from this that when you have a tough decision to make in life, trust your gut feeling. As it turned out, she never had another seizure the rest of her life. The best explanation we came up with was that, while she was at Lambs Farm for the few days, they did not give her water in the bowl and only provided water through a bottle attached to the cage. Sophie apparently did not drink any water out of the bottle. So the seizure as a puppy was attributed to dehydration from being without water for three or four days. Throughout her life, Sophie would drink more water than any other dog I knew. She was a sloppy drinker because of her long snout, and some water always spilled on the floor. She could easily drink two large bowls of water per day.

We also had to undo the initial boundary training we taught Sophie to not come into the kitchen. Sophie was a quick learner, and once she learned something, she would not forget it, or do the opposite very easily. We initially showed the boundary to the kitchen by walking Sophie up to the doorway, saying "no," and rewarding her with praise for staying in the family room. We never used a treat to reward expected or required behavior.

One instance of showing Sophie this rule remained firmly in her mind and she never crossed the barrier. Undoing the kitchen boundary after a month of her living with the rule was much harder to undo than teaching her to stay out to begin with. She would not come into the kitchen, no matter what coaxing we came up with. The kitchen floor was a wood floor and not carpeted. The family room was carpeted. To untrain Sophie, we put a small rug down, part in the kitchen and part in the family room. Each day we painstakingly moved it by three-inch increments into the kitchen. After several weeks, she was comfortable in the kitchen and we removed the rug.

We showed her the boundaries of the dining room and living room again and the upstairs to reinforce that it was okay to be in the kitchen. Again, showing her only one time, Sophie learned what it meant. I believe Lizzy also communicated the boundaries to her, as Lizzy had learned the boundaries from Brownie. We never taught them to Lizzy; only to Brownie. Neither Lizzy nor Sophie would come into the living or dining room, no matter how much you called them. Not teaching Sophie about the stairs and learning to use them would prove a problem later in life.

Some initial training of dogs can be taught much sooner and at a younger age than people think. There is no magic age of waiting until six months or longer before any training is started. The sooner you can start, the better. At a very young age, a puppy wants to be with you and follow you. This is the perfect time for them to be with you off-lead. Their brain is like a sponge, soaking up whatever you can teach them. I fully realized from the first day of training, Sophie was a fast learner. She recognized the usual dog commands of sit, stay, and down easily. Sophie was the kind of dog who did things for praise, not treats, so very little bribery was necessary.

In giving praise to a dog, most people would simply say, "good dog" or "good girl." I wanted to come up with a word that Sophie would normally not hear as part of everyday conversation or from anyone else. I settled on the word *excellent*, which Sophie was told to encourage her behavior when she was better than good. She thrived on the "excellent" behavior acclamation and knew she had done something special. She also knew I was the only person to reward her using the word "excellent."

During our first year together, I tried to spend an hour or so every day teaching Sophie. When it was too cold or rainy outside, I trained her inside. It may have been a shorter time on occasion, but I worked with her every day. This was a tremendous amount of time and time commitment, but Sophie was such an intelligent dog and so eager to please, I continued with the commitment. I saw her knowledge growing daily.

Sophie was not just a serious dog. She also had a playful side, especially in her younger years. Among her favorite things were going for long walks and picking up sticks. She would find a stick in the park we used for her runs and carry it as a treasure back to the house; the bigger the stick, the better. Sometimes it was a tree limb four to five feet in length. She would walk down the sidewalk, balancing it like a teeter-totter in her long snout. It was as if she found a prize, something she was so proud of and wanted to bring it home to show everyone.

Sophie liked to run in circles around the tree in the middle of our large backyard. We called it "Zooming" and used the command, "Sophie, ZOOM!" She would take off full speed and run circles around the tree. She ran so fast and made so much noise, it was as if you were watching a thoroughbred horse race. Sophie was pounding the turf, spinning out of the turn and coming into the stretch for home. She always ran in a counterclockwise direction, just like a horse race.

At the time we got Sophie, Lizzy was almost nine years old. Based on her smaller size, Lizzy was never that playful or an outdoor dog. Lizzy stood aside and watched Sophie but did not partake in carrying sticks or running around in circles.

Sophie's training also involved creating closeness between her and me so I could teach her to stay with me off-lead. We did not have a secure, fenced yard. In the entire first year of training, she only ran away once and returned quickly based on what she was taught as an "emergency recall." This required Sophie to stop and return immediately, as fast as she could run. Without a fence, training for recall was like walking a tight rope without a net; but the better Sophie did at staying by us, the more confidence she gained, and the more she listened to both my wife and me.

On Sophie's twice-a-day walks to the park I watched her become increasingly attentive to the things surrounding her. Although we saw squirrels, birds and rabbits, she never took off after them, even as a playful puppy. She noticed them and watched them but was not interested in going after them.

On several occasions, Sophie stopped to look at a rainbow. This is very unusual, especially for a young, active dog. On walks, she was most interested in the people around us, coming and going, and crossing the street. She wanted to see whoever else was around and meet and greet them. A few months after Sophie died, I was listening to a reading at church which described what everyone's behavior should be. The reading reminded me of things I saw in Sophie daily: kindness, humility, gentleness

34

and patience. Those qualities would be there from the start with Sophie. They were not taught by me, but part of the fabric of her personality. Over time, they became more noticeable and appreciated, especially her compassion and gentleness.

It was now time to get ready for the large crowd of forty for Thanksgiving dinner. After only two weeks of training, she was ready to meet the family crowd at the holiday. We created the same routine with people who came to our house that day. As we saw them coming down the sidewalk after getting out of their cars, I would take Sophie outside on the leash to meet and greet them. She was very proud to show herself off to a new friend and to respond to simple commands she had learned in the last several weeks. Everyone thought she was very cute and well behaved for a ten-week-old puppy.

Dogs like routine, and they like to fit into a certain behavior. Sophie was the perfect example of this. The families who came to Thanksgiving were a combination of old and middle-aged adults, and very young children. We taught Sophie to sit down and wait for each person to approach her and pet and praise her.

Jumping is common in puppies. Sophie was not prone to jumping on people at this young age or even later, so we never had to undo that behavior. Sophie learned to sit and wait for someone to approach her.

THANKSGIVING AT THE SLUPIK'S *		
YEAR	# OF ATTENDEES	TEMPERATURE
2001	40 + Sophie!	56
2000	34	37
1999	30	52
1998	36	65
1997	32	54
1996	33	39
1995	28	35
1994	25	52
1993	27	46
1992	25	38
1991	26	37
1990	27	54
1989	25	28
1988	28	60
1987	27	41
1986	28	37
1984	12	41
1982	28	36

*Data provided by Grandpa

Thanksgiving score card

Her good behavior at Thanksgiving made me think Sophie and I had another purpose in life. Her behavior and desire for human contact would help make her the perfect therapy dog.

Sophie was calm and interested in meeting and being petted by each person that day. Some of the smaller children who greeted her could be a little rough. They pulled her, grabbed her tail or pulled her ears. One child tried to ride her like a pony. I watched her closely that day out of concern that she might nip at someone. There never was a sign of any negative reaction or aggressiveness, even if a young child did something they shouldn't. Sophie knew it was a small, vulnerable child. If it was something Sophie did not enjoy, she would just walk away and go to the next person. This was an amazing disciplined behavior for a ten-week-old puppy.

Based on everyone playing with her, she became tired and wanted to have a nap. We put her in her crate for a nap, which just happened to coincide with Thanksgiving dinner. Even though there were forty people around her making noise, laughing, talking, and eating, she was out like a light in her crate for an hour and a half. The timing was perfect. She would continue to enjoy all the people at future Thanksgivings. Sophie thought the reason people came over to our home was to see her. That is why she made it her job to personally greet and learn about whoever came over.

We took Sophie to the vet the following week for a complete checkup and saw no signs of aftereffects from the one minor seizure. She appeared very healthy and continued to be healthy most of her life. She had problems the first year and last two years of her life, but many happy, healthy years in between. Our attention was about to be diverted to Lizzy, who was nine years old.

In December of 2001, we continued our tradition of cutting down a Christmas tree at a tree farm in Indiana. This tradition started many years earlier when our children were very young.

Annual trip to the Christmas tree farm

Our first dog, Brownie, went to the tree farm each year, and it was one of her favorite places. As a matter of fact, she enjoyed it so much that, after her passing in 1998, we spread her ashes at the Christmas tree farm. Each year, Lizzy went along to see the Christmas tree farm, but was never that fond of it. Whereas our children enjoyed the snow and cold, Lizzy did not. It seemed Lizzy was always cold, and we had to put a sweater on her and bundle her up inside my coat. She would look at me as if asking when it would be over.

This was the first year Sophie went to the Christmas tree farm with Lizzy. Sophie enjoyed the outside weather and the cold. She loved the snow, so it was a perfect place for her to go. Her initial trip to the Christmas tree farm was also her first experience with snow. We cut down our tree as usual and came back home to get ready for Christmas.

It was shortly after this that Lizzy had an accident climbing up some concrete stairs. Lizzy started to have trouble with her vision and appeared to mis-judge the depth of the steps. She banged both her back knees, fell, and was hurt rather badly. After a few days she was slightly better, but she was basically walking on three legs and not putting any pressure on the fourth one. We saw several vets (our regular vet and an orthopedic specialist), and they indicated that the injury looked pretty bad. Surgery was the only option to recovery, but that surgery might not work and most likely could prove fatal because Lizzy had a heart murmur issue. She would need to be confined to a crate for months after the surgery to aid the healing process. We had two different vets evaluate her, with the same conclusion.

We were torn as to whether to pursue the surgery based on her age. She was nine, and we thought that was old, but it really wasn't that old for a smaller dog. This was the first time we thought of an alternative medicine approach for our dogs. Alternative medicine treatment for dogs was very new at that point. We found a vet who did aqua-puncture, which was a combination of acupuncture and injecting Lizzy's knees with glucosamine. At this point Lizzy's luxating patellas (knees) were at stage 4. Stage 4 is as bad as it gets. Her joints were constantly going in and out of place.

After the first visit and treatment, Lizzy began to put pressure on the one hind leg she had not been using. After the second visit, she began to walk again. After the third visit a few days later, she was running. So in a matter of several weeks, we had not only avoided surgery (which may not have worked), but had brought her legs back to a much better shape. Although she would continue to need periodic injections the rest of her life, she lived to a ripe old age of sixteen and a half years. If we had listened to the regular vets, her life could have ended shortly after nine years. This was an awakening to look for alternative medicine, which we searched out particularly in the case of Sophie, as you will learn later.

With several months of treatment behind her, Lizzy seemed to get remarkably better. She was back to her young self, with no signs of any orthopedic problems. Her two favorite tricks were rolling over, which she did many times, and circling. She circled faster and faster in a counterclockwise method. She wasn't long enough to catch her tail, and we never knew why she did this. Especially since she did this circling in the same direction every time. We asked several vets if they had an explanation, and they did not. We researched it in several dog books and on the internet. In one book that we stumbled upon, this was called "mindless behavior." Lizzy was very simpleminded, which we again attributed to her being removed from her mother at five weeks.

Lizzy at age eleven fully recovered

Sophie's training continued on a daily basis, and at the age of six months, we enrolled her in her one and only obedience class. It was a class for new puppies at a training center called Narnia. The first day of class, there were fourteen dogs and owners who were required to come to the first session. The start of the session consisted of the dogs standing around in a circle, while the trainer in the middle of the circle spoke for about ten minutes, summarizing what the objectives of the class would be. Sophie was the only dog to sit perfectly still at my side and not bark during the ten-minute introduction. Sophie was looking at the trainer and appeared to be absorbing the conversation intensely.

After ten minutes of lecture, the trainer suggested we let the dogs off-lead to let them run off some energy and get to know each other. Every dog but Sophie went to the center of the room and started barking and chasing the other dogs. It was quite chaotic, but Sophie did not participate. She was much more interested in people than dogs. Sophie took it upon herself to walk around the room in a clockwise circle and introduce herself to every owner standing in the circle. One by one she went up to them, poked them with her nose, got a pet, and then went on to the next person. You could probably not even train a dog to do this, or if you did, it would take a lot of practice. Sophie's behavior at six months was remarkable. It was my opinion that she wanted to meet all these people and make sure they knew who she was. It was moments like this that we began to realize what a special dog Sophie was and what special place she might take.

It was obvious she had much affection for people, and that confirmed my thinking of potentially training her to be a therapy dog. She was interested in people, observant, and seemed to be able to invoke a reaction from everyone she visited.

The rest of the six weeks of class was rather boring for Sophie. Sophie already knew the basics of puppy obedience. Not only did she know all of the verbal commands, I had begun to teach her hand signals. She knew many of the commands by hand signals without words: sit, stay, down, come, and speak. The hand signals were ones I made up and not from any official book, and I came to learn most of them were very unorthodox. But she learned them and she retained them for life. I learned that if a dog knows hand signals, they are much more attentive in watching their owner, and looking to their owner constantly for direction. I used the same hand signals with my subsequent dogs, and even in training and observing therapy dogs, which I now do as a volunteer.

It was time for Sophie's six-month checkup, at which time she received certain shots, and was put on heart guard and flea protection. Subsequent to this six-month checkup, Sophie began getting a neurological illness every three or four weeks. She couldn't walk, couldn't hold her head up, and vomited. We went through this for several months, doing various treatments with the vet we started with. They ran special tests, and we spent $3,000, finding out nothing. Sophie did not seem to get any better and was on a schedule of a cycle of three to four weeks with this illness. We wanted another vet opinion and chose the University of Wisconsin Veterinary School in Madison. Upon entering the campus, a sign told us that "large animals" were to the left and small animals were to the right. I followed the large-animal sign, thinking that Sophie was rather large for a dog. I soon learned that "large animals" meant horses and cows.

The vet hospital in Madison seemed to us like the Mayo Clinic for dogs. We made an appointment and took Sophie early one morning and began to talk to the vet students and the vets. After two hours of tests and questions, we explained the symptoms and what was happening. Sophie sat patiently and let the team of vet students exam her extensively.

One of the vets came in and asked if we were giving Sophie Heartgard. We answered, "Of course we give it to her, as it was prescribed by our vet." After all, we were good, responsible pet owners wanting to make sure our dog got what she required. It turned out you cannot give collies Heartgard medications! We had no idea the medications and treatment we were giving her for heartworm protection was causing the problem. So every month, we had been giving her a pill that started a downward spiral for a week.

Collies have one less chromosome than other dogs and are not tolerant of Heartgard and the ivermectin in it. Most vets know this, especially today, but at the time the vet that we were going to had no familiarity with collies. Upon being told of an alternative to Heartgard, Sophie recovered, and all of the symptoms ceased to exist. This was at about nine months of age, and her health was now under control.

To celebrate Lizzy's resurgence and Sophie's recovery, we decided to take a dog vacation, visiting places where only dogs were allowed. Both dogs were excellent car riders. We had purchased a Tahoe because we needed a bigger vehicle for Sophie. Lizzy had a special seat on the console. Sophie was in the back with the seats down and folded flat. Sophie was level with the windows and had a 360-degree panoramic view outside the car. We spent a little over a week driving to various locations, mostly in Wisconsin. We stayed at places that allowed dogs and went to parks that allowed dogs. Almost every activity was concentrated on being able to do something with our dogs. We certainly were a little crazy for having done this, but the two dogs thoroughly enjoyed themselves. They enjoyed walks on the beach, walks in the park, walks along Lake Michigan, and visiting zoos.

Lizzy and Sophie got our constant attention for over a week. After the vacation, we came home and restarted daily training with Sophie.

It was then that I learned about a pet therapy dog program at a local hospital. The hospital had started to allow therapy dogs to visit patients. After submitting an application, the program required an initial evaluation for temperament, and then four

Sophie and a cold Lizzy on the shores of Lake Michigan

Sophie visiting a zoo while on vacation

Guess who got to sit in the hammock?

different sessions to train and test the dog. Sophie was approaching her one-year birthday, and this was the minimum requirement for testing to become a therapy dog.

Most of the people I talked to advised me not to test immediately, as it was a hard test. They thought Sophie was most likely to fail at that young age. This did not deter me or Sophie from proceeding and trying the test. Sophie's intelligence and responses to my training gave us the confidence to try it. In addition to family and friends, our pet walker was part of this program, and said there is no possible way Sophie could pass the test.

I believe if you have confidence in your dog and yourself, you are capable of many great things together. The same applies to life situations. The more confidence you have in yourself, the more you succeed. You need to show confidence, even when you may not have it. I had confidence in what Sophie had learned, and she never disappointed me. We were about to prove everyone wrong. She would become the youngest active dog at the local hospital's certified therapy dog program. A coincidence? I think not.

A Year of Training Pays Off

Shortly after Sophie's first birthday, she was eligible to try out for the hospital therapy dog program. The trial for interested dogs and handlers was held at the hospital one day in the late fall of 2002.

The program started earlier in the year and seemed to generate a lot of success stories. The idea was new in our area and in most parts of the country. Stories were published about the tryouts in the local newspaper and generated more participation and interest. Of one hundred dogs temperament tested when Sophie and I tried out, only sixteen qualified and were selected for the second round. The second round was four full days of intensive training for the program.

The purpose of temperament testing measures the dog's reactions in different unpredictable circumstances. The dogs also had to have general obedience, but not necessarily specific commands such as heeling. It was more important to see how the dogs reacted to different situations, and recovered from a misdeed or a surprise, if necessary. In other words, a dog could make a mistake and not be disqualified. What was more important was the dog's reaction to the mistake, the handler's reaction, and the appropriate recovery.

Each dog was tested individually for about ten minutes. The testing team set up an obstacle course for the dogs to walk through to see their reactions to various startling distractions. Along the obstacle course the helpers made loud noises by banging pots, jumping out from behind a screen, or trying to take the dog from the handler.

As we waited our turn, I could see Sophie intently watching the dog before her so she could be ready for anything. The dogs were not permitted to bark or show any aggression toward the testers who were surprising or scaring them. There was also testing of basic commands. I chose to have Sophie walk with me off-lead for most of these tests. The testers were surprised that a dog this young would stay that closely with me and listen to me off-lead (without a leash). When I did recall her, she instantly came to me, sat in front of me and "finished" by walking around my left side and sitting as if at an AKC dog show. Sophie had learned her basic commands very well.

We went home to await results. We found out the following week that Sophie was one of the dogs who passed the temperament test and was selected for the four days of further training. The training would be conducted on Saturdays and Sundays on two consecutive weekends.

After the temperament testing, the training was done at the hospital by a registered nurse who started the program, several helpers, and the certified therapy dog tester to assist in the control and observations. We all met for the first time. Sixteen dogs that were unfamiliar with each other in a relatively small area could create havoc. As usual, Sophie was the best behaved, in addition to being the youngest in the room. It was as if she completely understood the purpose of the training before it happened and took it on as a job she needed to learn. I soon found out I needed to learn more about the rules and procedures than Sophie did.

One of the helpers during the training was our pet walker. The pet walker had a female Cavalier King Charles dog that was part of the initial batch of qualified dogs earlier that year. I never knew if she really believed Sophie and I would not pass the test, or if she was a little jealous that Sophie would be in the program at such a young age.

In the first few years of the animal assisted therapy program, the training was quite extensive, requiring a commitment of time and obligation that most volunteers would be hesitant to do. In later years, as we remained in part of the program, the training course would be cut down to less than two days. I am not sure if a decision was made that all of that training was not necessary, or if to some extent the program was made easier to attract more volunteers with less training time requirements. In the beginning, the hospital was very cautious from a liability standpoint and wanted to have the right dogs. More time was spent training the handler.

It was obvious to me that some people volunteered for the wrong reasons. Some people volunteered so they could tell everyone they were a volunteer. You should volunteer with a commitment to accomplish something for the organization you signed up for, not for recognition or to be able to tell your friends about it. Over the years, some of the dogs who passed the test and were certified lasted less than three months in the program.

They quit when they realized the level of commitment required to complete three hours of visiting per time.

I do not think that shortcutting the training as the trainers did later in the program was a good decision. I believe the quality of dogs that were added to the program in later years was not close to the quality of the initial dogs in the program.

The four days of training simulated actual hospital visits. A person was in a hospital bed, people were walking in and out of the room, and the handler and dog practiced entering a room to meet the patient, reacting with the patient, talking to the patient, meeting visitors, and exiting the room. This basic procedure was practiced over and over, with suggestions for both the handler and dog from the tester/observer.

The dogs were not allowed to come into the room without the patient in the room saying it was okay. This was a double-check of the list of patients to visit that the handler received upon arriving at the hospital. The most important thing for practice was that the dog paid attention to the handler's commands. The dog had to be engaged with the handler throughout the hospital, going from room to room. The dog and handler waited at the patient's room door until they were granted entrance. Dogs were not permitted to bark at any time during the visit or to take any food from the patient. Part of the training was for handlers to be ready for different situations, and to maintain control of the dog throughout the visit. Most important was that the dog did not run off within the hospital, for this could create a dangerous situation.

As the days continued, work on the exercises got more complicated. One of the exercises was to put the sixteen dogs that were being tested in the circle in the center of the room. The dogs were put in a down stay with no lead, and the handlers walked back about ten feet away from the dogs. I never knew why this was part of the hospital therapy test, as rules for therapy dogs require they keep their distance from each other while working, a minimum of two feet away. I have never seen this test in any other dog training.

While the dogs were in the center circle, testers first walked around them, attempting to disturb them. They walked around the dogs with canes, then crutches, then wheelchairs. When they got to the wheelchair, the trainer would drop the wheelchair at the outside of the circle. Two of the dogs scattered with canes, two scattered with crutches, and nine scattered with the dropping of the first wheelchair. Sophie remained in the center of the circle with two other dogs. Two of the other trainers then took wheelchairs and walked around the three remaining dogs. Both wheelchairs were tossed down at the same time near the dogs. The other two dogs got up and ran. Sophie was the only dog remaining in stay. Sophie almost challenged the trainers to do something to force her to get up.

For the final round, both testers took wheelchairs and circled around Sophie and tossed them quite closely, more so than I think should be considered safe. Sophie basically looked at the testers with astonishment, as if to ask them, "What are you doing?" She got up, moved about a foot, and laid back down with them as if to say, "I am not going to move until my owner releases me." Sophie passed the test with flying colors.

We trained each day from 9:00 a.m. to 4:00 p.m. The final exam was in the afternoon on the fourth day. The dogs and handlers were tired, and the dogs were not permitted to have lunch or any treats for the day and only had a short water break around lunchtime. To pass the final test, the dog had to walk across a forty-foot room that was filled with dog food and dog biscuits on the floor. This exercise was conducted with the dog off-lead at the handler's side and walking slowly across the floor. The purpose of the test was to assure that the dog would not eat or lick anything on the hospital floor, as it could be dangerous. They did not want a dog licking blood or eating medicine accidentally dropped on the floor.

Sophie responded perfectly and did not reach for any food. One of the first commands Sophie had learned was "off," and she knew it well. I could put a dog biscuit six inches from her nose, tell her "off," and she would not take it until you released her to take it.

After the food test, we went around to different rooms of the hospital led by a tester as the tester checked and evaluated fifty different items. I would learn after the fact that both the handler and the dog were being graded at the same time. Sophie and I were graded on fifty items, and there were three errors on that final exam. Our grade was an A+. The three mistakes? They were all classified as "handler errors." Sophie was getting a perfect score at a very young age that amazed everyone. She was on her way to becoming a very good therapy dog.

Up until that point, Sophie was very serious during the training. Supposedly, collies need a job in life, and pet therapy was going to be Sophie's specialty. After walking out of the room with Sophie, knowing we passed, I asked her to jump up on me and she put her front paws on my chest, and we gave each other hugs in that emotional moment. She had succeeded beyond my wildest expectations, and was easily the best dog in the class. She was joining a group of almost twenty dogs that passed earlier in the year. Over twelve and a half years of therapy work, I never met a dog that was as good at her job and connected to patients, family, and staff as well as Sophie.

On graduation day, the ceremony was held in the lobby of the hospital. Present was the nurse who started the program, various trainers, the handlers and dogs, and family and friends. In addition, some of the successful handlers and dogs from previous classes were there. It was very crowded in this area of the hospital, and there was almost not enough room for everyone to stand. It was almost like a final test of the dogs, as they were put in a close situation with many people and dogs.

Graduation Day!

My family came to Sophie's graduation as if it was a child's graduation. A group of young children played the traditional graduation march, "Pomp and Circumstance," on the piano. My wife was there, along with my son Dan, and our daughter-in-law Stacey, and my niece Pam, and her husband Wayne. We still look at the pictures today and treasure that moment of Sophie passing and earning her certificate. We all knew that she was the best. It was a formal graduation, and they called the dog's name to come up and get their diploma.

The nurse awarding the diplomas stepped up onto a small landing in the lobby of the hospital for the dogs to come up to get their diploma. I had not even thought it, but for a year, Sophie was trained to never go up the stairs. So here it was her time to go up and get her diploma, and she would not go up the stairs. The audience thought it was funny, but I knew what caused it. It had nothing to do with the day's events. It rather had to do with the training at home and telling her one time that she was not allowed to go up the stairs.

As soon as graduation was over, I knew I would have to go about untraining this behavior. In the hospital that had five floors, if an elevator did not work and there was an emergency or fire, you must rely on the stairs. It was much harder to undo the training of not going up stairs than it was to initially train her that lesson. How Sophie would have remembered for a year without reinforcing it on a regular basis was quite amazing. When I called her, she looked at me as if to say, "You should know better, I am not allowed on stairs."

Now that graduation was complete, we were assigned to a team (initially a total of three people but eventually four). Our first visits started the following week. We chose Friday night to work, as there was a shortage of people who wanted to volunteer on Friday night.

We developed quite a relationship with some of the people on Friday nights, which you will find out about later in this book. So now, I'm on to the first visit which again would be a remarkable coincidence; or, maybe it was not.

CHAPTER 5

The First Therapy Visit

In early 2003 we received Sophie's diploma, and we were ready to do our first visit. I chose to visit the hospital on Friday nights, as it worked best with my work schedule. If I learned anything over time, it forced me to leave the office a little bit earlier, go home to feed Sophie, and get ready to start her visits at six o'clock. This is a great life lesson Sophie taught me, that you can and should make time for what is important to you.

As part of the first several dog therapy groups, we typically spent at least two and a half hours, if not three hours, at the hospital on Friday nights. Initially, teams were three volunteers; but some nights in the early years, there were less, as every volunteer was not always available on their assigned night. As the number of dogs in the program continued to grow, eventually up to a total of between eighty and ninety, the length of time that Sophie and I were required to be at the hospital was less. Based on Sophie's energetic attitude and personality, we just expanded the time spent in each room if four dogs were on duty and not just three.

There were very special rules for both the handler and the dog once you entered the hospital. For a volunteer handler and dog, this was a lot to learn and maintain. Sophie liked routine, and was a perfect student of the rules. The volunteer handler wore a blue hospital coat with an identification tag that contained their name and picture. The dogs also had an identification tag with their picture, just as any other hospital employee.

Hospital I.D. tags

Sophie and I had to stand in line and get our pictures taken together at graduation for a plaque that would hang in the main lobby of the hospital. The plaque, which consisted of a picture of the handler and dog, was placed on the hospital wall once they commenced the program and obtained a sponsor. The sponsor made a $500 contribution to the program.

Based on the plaque funding requirement, Sophie had to earn her plaque and her place on the wall before her picture was put up. Fortunately, Sophie already had made a lot of friends who

Graduation plaque

were anxious to be her sponsor, and her plaque went up almost immediately after graduation.

The therapy dog guidelines of the hospital were very strict, and Sophie was excellent at following rules, but we still had to work out a routine in the initial year of visits. It took a few months and about one hundred visits to work out how we conducted our visits. Sophie knew we were going to visit as soon as she saw my blue coat and her tag. Sophie understood the word "visit," and her ears tilted forward at the sound of that word. Collies, as a herding dog breed, like to work and like to have a job, and Sophie viewed the visits at the hospital as her most important job. It was a long way from her natural instinct of sheep herding, but she learned it well.

Upon entering the main entrance of the hospital on Friday night, we would go up to the volunteer office on the third floor. This required a trip up the elevator, which Sophie enjoyed the first time we tried it. There was specific elevator etiquette that had to be followed, including going to the back of the elevator, turning around and having the dog sit. Also, you never entered an elevator with a dog without the permission of the other occupants first.

To get around in the hospital, we mostly used the elevators. Once you are in the elevator, you had to stand quietly in a corner until your floor came up, and then excuse yourself to get off the elevator. Sophie had neither problems nor reactions to getting on or off the elevators.

The stairs, however, were another adventure. I had to work with her for about three months at the hospital, either before or after we visited patients, to get her used to the stairs going up and down. She eventually overcame her either fear of stairs or her previous knowledge that she wasn't supposed to be on them.

It could be important. Especially in the instance of a hospital emergency, if there was a fire or power outage, we had to be able to get out of the building. The dogs and the handlers also had to take part in a safety class each year to learn different things at the hospital to do or not to do, in case of an emergency. It seemed a bit of overkill, as my first reaction to a fire would be to find a way out for Sophie and myself.

As part of the four days of training, we had toured the entire hospital, including the adjoining buildings and all floors, to become familiar with all areas. Therefore, by the day of the first visit, Sophie was pretty well acquainted with which floors the dogs were allowed on and where they were located. As the hospital grew and the program grew, there were many more floors to visit. Over our time at the hospital, it almost doubled in size.

If you were assigned a day shift, you were also allowed to visit in places like the emergency room waiting area, or the patient recovery area where visitors would be. Those places were usually not allowed as visits at night. For almost our entire time at the hospital, we worked on Friday nights and no other time. We got to know quite a few different handlers and dogs. Many of the handlers have since become good friends from that experience, even though their dogs have passed away. A few of them remained in the program with a different dog, but most quit after the first dog retired from service.

We gathered in the volunteer office on Friday until all the team members were present and ready to go to work. We divided the areas to be visited amongst us and usually took at least two floors apiece. There were thirty-two beds on a floor, or sixty-four total for two floors. Almost all the rooms were private, which improved the quality of the visit. Sometimes either nurses or other visitors left a note for our team asking to see a certain patient who had a favorite dog. This actually was quite common in the beginning. When patients were admitted to the hospital, they were asked (at admission) if they would like to see a therapy dog as part of their stay. It was part of the intake form and the patient medical file. Sometimes the question was missed. Some nurses were better than others about asking people to see a dog.

On our first night working at the hospital, we had a situation with a man who had been hospitalized after being attacked by a dog. When he saw us walking through the hall, he asked for a visit. He had had a collie as a child who was a very gentle and compassionate companion. After clearing it with the charge nurse, we walked in, and Sophie could not have been kinder and gentler to him. Sophie made him feel like a kid again and helped start his healing process. I believe Sophie started or sped up the healing process for many of the people she visited. Somehow she always had a sense of which person to do what with and pay more attention to. It was amazing that she could visit a man who had been admitted for dog bites and take away his fear of dogs.

Over the years, one of the floors we always worked on with Sophie was the orthopedic floor. Most patients on the floor had been admitted for knee and hip or back surgery. Smaller dogs were allowed to be put on the bed if a patient requested, but this was not practical with orthopedic patients.

My group on Friday nights usually contained small dogs. That meant that Sophie and I would do the visits for the orthopedic floor almost every time. Sophie was a "table top" dog, as her head was even with the patient's bed, and it was not necessary to put her on the bed. The patients could touch and interact with Sophie easily, even while sitting up in their bed. The common denominator of the orthopedic floor was that it had mostly older patients, in their sixties, seventies, or eighties. The oldest patient Sophie and I saw was ninety-six years old. Many of these patients remembered having a collie as a child or on a farm or most certainly from the movie or the television show *Lassie*. Sophie's coloring and markings were very similar to Lassie, although she was probably slightly bigger than most female collies. Sophie was the size of the male collie, Pal, who played the original Lassie.

When working in the hospital, the preference was for the dog to be in a heeling position as she walked down the hall and into and out of the rooms. The dog was required to sit at the entrance of the room before going in to visit. Although we always started with a list of people who wanted to see dogs based on the nurses questioning them, sometimes the patient may have changed their mind, or sometimes they were admitted without asking the question of whether or not they wanted to see the dog. If that was the case, we were required to check with the charge nurse for their room, and have that patient added to the computer list eligible for a dog visit, and then get permission to enter the room.

Part of the process of a visit with patients was also a visit with the patient's family and guests. Whether they were in the hallway or in the room itself, and especially visiting on a Friday night, there were many visitors. We would walk into the room, introduce Sophie, talk to the patient briefly and then go over to visitors in the room. If they wanted to see her, she made it her job to go down the line visitor to visitor until she had introduced herself to everyone in the room. We would then circle back to the patient, and most times Sophie would be able to sit at the patient's side with her head above the bed, and the patient would be able to talk to her and pet her without having to reach down.

We also had many encounters with nurses and doctors. Almost all of the nurses were very positive about the program and fond of Sophie. Sophie would recognize those nurses over time and go up to greet them and thank them for assisting in this service. The nurses and staff were even more likely, in later years, to seek us out, as they had come to know and admire Sophie for her work. Everyone knew Sophie by name. Even though my name tag was as big as Sophie's, the staff usually knew me as "Sophie's owner." The orthopedic nurses went out of their way to make sure Sophie saw the most people on their floor. Whereas the typical floor had thirty-two beds, many of the other floors may have had requests for dog visits by four or five patients on that floor. On the orthopedic floor, we usually had a minimum of twelve to fourteen patients who wanted to see a dog, and in some cases up to twenty. Based on requests, on one of our typical Friday nights, twenty out of twenty-four patients on the floor requested to see Sophie.

The nurses were very kind to us. If they saw a patient who had not yet requested to see a dog, and it was Sophie's night to work, they would do a double-check with the patients who had not signed up for a visit. Oftentimes, a family member present would see Sophie and me pass by the room and encourage a visit. Part of the interest may have also been in older patients who had no visitors. Although at the time they were asked, the patient usually had no idea which dog was going to visit.

Many handlers and dogs went through the visits without any emotion. This would never be the case with Sophie.

Sophie and I had encounters with doctors and staff that would be in patient rooms, at which time we would usually say we could come back later. At other times, the staff would be in a patient's room and invite us to come in. Most of them were very supportive of the program; and in later years not only did the nurses know Sophie by name, but many doctors knew her by name as well. Almost no doctor remembered my name. Doctors would meet Sophie once and still remember her name years later. She must have made quite an impression on them.

Sophie also came to know all the people at the front desk of the hospital (the concierge desk) and the various help desks throughout the hospital. In the initial years, the hospital allowed a therapy dog to go anywhere in the hospital that the staff could. So we had gone to nurses' employee lounges, the doctors' lounge, and even the cafeteria line.

It was quite amusing the few times I had to go straight to the hospital from work without eating dinner, and we would stop at the cafeteria for a quick snack. People saw a large dog moving along the buffet line almost pushing a tray. They were astonished. I think Sophie was one of the few dogs in the cafeteria line, as most therapy dog visits were done in the morning or mid-afternoon. After about a year or two of allowing therapy dogs in the cafeteria, the hospital thought better of this and changed the policy. Dogs were no longer allowed to go through the food line. They still were allowed to sit in the cafeteria while a person ate, but obviously the handler could not leave them unattended. I think Sophie enjoyed walking through the line and looking at all the food, more than eating it.

Once in a patient's room, we were not allowed to assist the patient in any way or give the patient anything. If the patient needed something or needed help immediately, we would have to leave the room and call the charge nurse. The patients were not allowed to offer their food to the dogs. Although many patients eating dinner offered Sophie a bite of their supper, the food would be a distraction.

I believe the hospital was mostly afraid of dogs having an accident while visiting patients. There was a special rule of who to call and what to do to clean up if your dog had an accident. Fortunately, Sophie never had an accident at the hospital. Some of the handlers would take a break midway through their visiting schedule, and take the dog outside and bring the dog back in. We never needed to do this and never left the hospital once we started our visiting routine.

While walking through the hospital, Sophie and I were approached by many people for special requests, such things as "my mom would like to see a dog"; or "my dad had collies when he was growing up, so please come and see us." We would walk into the room to ask the people if they wanted to see Sophie. Many times, they were on the phone and they would tell their caller, "I have to hang up now; I have to see this collie in my room. I will call you back later." In the beginning of the program, most people were not aware that the hospital even allowed dogs in the room.

Our good friend, Linda, was in the hospital for a short stay, and we went to see her shortly after her surgery and recovery as a surprise visit with Sophie. We were allowed to make special visits on a non-scheduled workday, as long as we followed the rules and protocol of visits. Linda laughed and interacted with Sophie and thoroughly enjoyed the visit. Sophie was very surprised to see someone she knew in the bed. I never knew a dog could make you laugh, but Sophie sure did, as you can see from the picture below. After we left her, Linda fell asleep and woke up again in about an hour. When her husband came to visit, Linda told him the story that she thought she was dreaming that Sophie had come to see her. Her husband, Larry, thought she might be hallucinatory from the anesthetic and was about to question her nurse. In fact, it was not a dream, but the real thing. Once again, Sophie started the healing process.

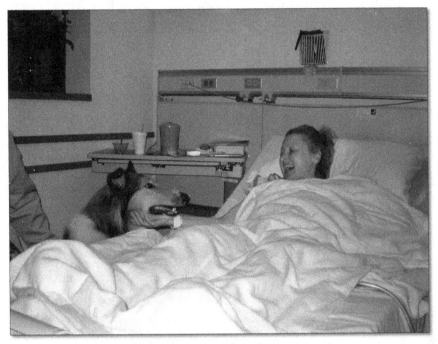

Sophie visiting with her friend, Linda

Sometimes people (patients or visitors) were eating when we walked into the room. When people were eating, we would mention that we could come back at a later time. Most of the people wanted to see Sophie so much that they stopped eating and pushed their food aside. Other times, after the visit, people would ask us to come back in an hour, when their spouse was there, or their grandchildren were there, or any other friend who would love a dog. Not only did they want to see Sophie the first time that night, they wanted us to come back to show her off to their family and friends if they were coming later that night. It was these kinds of requests that kept us late many times on a Friday night. After a while, my wife came to expect us being late and did not even call looking for us.

Sophie could establish a bond with people within a few minutes. Once you met Sophie, you had the feeling that you had known her forever.

When Sophie first came up to a patient, she would pay intense attention to them and react to what they said or did, or if they petted her. Sometimes a patient didn't seem to want to converse or pet her. Sophie would go up to them and nudge their hand or their arm at the side of the bed with her collie nose until they paid attention to her. It was like she was saying, "I am here to help you, so you better start paying attention to me." Patients were curious about Sophie. They asked where she came from, how old she was, and how hard it was to do this type of training and work.

Our hardest therapy days of our career at the hospital came in our first year of service. Several times on a Friday night when three people were scheduled, Sophie and I were the only team able to make it. We tried our best, but still could not make it to all the patients in the hospital who wanted to see a dog. The first time this happened, we stayed for over three and a half hours, and still could not see everyone. At that point, I decided it was long enough, we did the best we could, and we went home. Even though Sophie was a young dog, after that extra-long session of visiting, the next day she was sick all day. It was too much stress for one dog in a short period of time. Her concentration level was intense, and she paid attention to anyone and everything around her. This was her job, and she was going to do the best she could do with it.

In the early years, some people had cameras and wanted to take Sophie's picture. With the advent of cell phones and pictures on smart phones, many people wanted a picture of Sophie with them in their room or with their family. Sophie was even part of a few selfies. She was a beautiful dog and knew to smile when her picture was being taken. I don't know how she learned to smile, because I did not teach her; but in almost every picture she was in from about a couple years of old to her passing, she was smiling. If you look closely at most of the pictures in this book, you will see that Sophie is indeed smiling.

Sophie smiling at age twelve

Sophie was a content and happy dog. If we could all only be that happy and satisfied with our work, this would be a much better place for everyone around us. Her secret was doing something she loved to do, and people loved her to do it.

As previously mentioned, another part of the program had been making the equivalent of a baseball trading card of the dogs to leave behind with the patient, especially for their children or grandchildren. This became quite popular over the years, and patients who were in the hospital for days enjoyed collecting the cards. I used to tease the patients that if they could stay at the hospital for a month, they would be able to collect most of the dog cards from each dog that visited. Patients would put the dog cards on the bulletin board in their room and always want extras of Sophie's card for family members. If they were in the hospital several days, they would have several dogs' cards on their bulletin board. We usually asked about the previous dogs who visited, and most times the patient would tell us they enjoyed Sophie visiting them the most. Handlers who visited after Sophie would tell me stories of how much the patients enjoyed Sophie. She could connect with the patients over a very short time. I know there are real people who can heal others. I have no way of proving it, but I believe Sophie could heal both emotionally and physically. There have been studies that have shown patients who have had dog visits used less pain medication and had shorter stays. Sophie had that talent.

As the first few years went along, Sophie and I gained confidence in each of our abilities. It was like she and I were on the same wavelength and knew when to extend the visit and knew when to cut it short with a person who was not up to a long visit. Sometimes we would go to several patients, and none of them would be anxious to see us. Perhaps they were in pain or depressed. It's not that we got rejected a lot, but it did happen on occasion.

At other times, with a special visit, we extended our stay well beyond the average five to six minutes per room. Some visits turned into fifteen to twenty minutes. Some visits had two parts, an initial meeting for the day, completing her rounds, and then coming back to that room to spend more time with the patient. We had many special visits, especially with older people who were not only sick, but had no family and were lonely.

During our first year, I remember one of our special visits with an older woman in her seventies named Margaret who originated from Scotland, and had raised collies as a child. (The collie breed originated in Scotland.) Margaret smiled warmly when she first saw Sophie, as she was remembering her youth. This is something I won't forget. We probably spent forty-five minutes with her that night. We talked about her collies as a kid

Sophie checking out her plaque

and how she trained them and what she named them. It was as if she had been transported back to her childhood and Sophie was one of her dogs. The following week, when we came back, she had been discharged. It was a moment in time when she and Sophie connected. I remember her crying and thanking us as we left her room. We never saw her again. But that one night was a special memory to treasure: watching Sophie create so much happiness by her mere presence. Coincidence? I think not.

Among our Friday night group, the rule was if anyone asked for a special breed and we were it, we would make the extra visit to that patient at the end of the night. So some patients got two visits, one from the first dog scheduled for their floor and the second from their special dog they requested.

Over the years, requests for Sophie as the special dog were much more frequent than the requests for other dogs. Since a collie was not that common, whenever someone ran into a patient who had a collie at one time in their life, Sophie and I always made a special visit. In later years, even the nurses began to look forward to Sophie's visits on Friday, as we did. They could tell from the patients' comments and reactions how important the visit was. Sophie was visiting a friend of the family within a minute or two of first contact with the patient. I was amazed that a bond and a memory could be formed in such a short period of time.

CHAPTER 6

Sophie Dophie

Even though Sophie was serious and attentive about her job, she was also a playful puppy. She was like a young child, learning something every day. Her silly streak showed she enjoyed having fun, and shortly after Sophie came home with us, I nicknamed her Sophie Dophie. I even called her Dophie for a while, until I realized she wanted to be called Sophie.

I learned later that there was a famous collie in Scotland in the 1800s named Sophie Dophie. Sophie Dophie even has her own blog and website. So, it was a complete accident that I came up with that name.

Sophie wanted to be occupied all the time, because I believe she was so intelligent. She became bored if she did not have an activity to do. She was taken on lots of walks; usually a morning and an evening walk by me and a midday walk by a dog walker. Her walks provided lots of exercise and helped release some of her excess energy as a puppy.

On her walks, Sophie knew things instinctively that I never had to teach her. If someone was behind us walking briskly and catching up to us, we would move to the side to let them pass. Sophie enjoyed and appreciated the outdoors, and was not going to be rushed. Anytime we saw something unusual, we would stop and watch. This was our quiet time; not much conversation and absolutely no cell phone, email, or texting.

During the day, Sophie was left home with Lizzy, the Chihuahua. Lizzy was very passive and Sophie was very attentive to her. Even though Sophie weighed fifteen times more than Lizzy, Lizzy was alpha over Sophie. The dogs were not crated during the day. They were confined to a certain area of the house when we were gone, which included a long hallway, laundry room, and a fairly large family room. The dogs honored the boundaries without gates or formal restrictions. When at home, I would try to call them to come into the living or dining rooms as a test; they would not enter the room.

The family room had windows on both the front and back of the room. The front windows could be used to look down the street and see what was happening on our block, a twelve-house-long cul-du-sac street. The back windows, which were floor-to-ceiling windows, looked out into our backyard, which was quite big and about 350 feet across at the back of the yard. We had many squirrels, chipmunks, and birds, almost a zoo of wild animals to entertain Sophie. She would sit and watch them and monitor what they were doing. She was never a dog who wanted to chase squirrels or chipmunks or rabbits or even bark at them. She would just be aware of them.

On her walks, Sophie looked at birds and trees, but she was always more interested in the people on the street, the people around her, and the cars passing by. When we went on a walk, she wanted to meet everyone we passed. Over the years, many of the neighborhood children, as well as the parents, got to know Sophie. Rain or shine, hot or cold, snow or dry, Sophie would go on her walk. The weather could be absolutely unbearable, but nothing stopped our walks.

Sophie loved the snow, and I still remember the pleasure she had discovering the snow at three months old. Sophie ran and bounced and rolled in the snow and even tasted it. She did not mind the cold, of course, based on being a collie with her natural fur coat. We would have to put a sweater on Lizzy the Chihuahua in the winter, but Sophie never really needed anything to protect her until she was much older. In later years, her coat did not seem as thick, so we bought her a raincoat to help in the cold rain or the severe cold of winter

She never got her leash tangled around a tree or bush or tried to come around the other way and wrap the leash around the trunk. I did not teach her this, but I will say of all the other dogs I have had, no one knew it by instinct as Sophie did.

Sophie was excellent at meeting dogs along the way and being friendly with them. She didn't show any sign of aggression, even if the other dog did. On our block, one of the neighbors owned a small white hairless Chihuahua named Lilly. The neighbor let Lilly run loose without a leash and would sometimes lose control over her. Once Lilly came running across the street as I was walking Sophie, and barreled into Sophie, broadsiding her, biting her and pulling on Sophie's fur. This little dog was lucky that Sophie did not retaliate. Sophie shook Lilly off and looked at her as if to say, "You are crazy . . . and you better not do that again!"

Sophie never growled at another person or dog. The only time I saw her big white canine teeth was when a stray coyote approached us in a field near our home. That night, Sophie was not going to let that coyote get near me. We never saw the coyote again. Sophie also would share her food with either humans, if they wanted it (no thank you, Sophie) or with

Riding in the car, looking out

another dog. Initially this was the case with Lizzy. Sophie would also share her rawhide with Lizzy. Lizzy had a smaller mouth and little teeth and enjoyed it once Sophie had softened it up a bit for her.

Sophie learned to go everywhere with us, as would Lizzy most of the time. They both loved the car and wanted to be with us. Sophie enjoyed looking out the side windows; Lizzy rode in a small cat bed on the console of our Chevrolet Tahoe and enjoyed looking out the front window.

On occasion we would roll down the window and let Sophie put her head out if we were in local traffic. She was a very long dog, and from the car behind it looked as if she were half out the window, when she really wasn't. It is probably not the best thing to allow a dog to do, and there are probably many hazards to doing that while moving. But she loved looking out almost all the time she spent in the car.

When Sophie was six, I purchased a 1959 Ford Galaxy with a retractable hardtop that I wanted to restore. It was an amazing piece of engineering from the 1950s, with sixteen motors and relays lifting up the hard top and stowing it into the trunk. The car was rose colored with a large interior space, a parade seat, and a 440-horsepower Thunderbird engine.

In addition to the whole family, Sophie wanted to try it out. With the wind in her face and thousands of smells to smell, Sophie got her ride. She was as excited as a child with her first ride in a convertible. It was quite windy in the back seat while rolling along at 55+ mph.

She liked the car so much that she would sit in the back seat in the driveway, waiting for us to take her for a ride if she found the car door open.

With the wind in her face . . .

Waiting for her ride

We took Sophie to the office on a regular basis where she would wait and greet clients at the front door. In later years, she would fall asleep at the front door, and only wake up when someone came in. She might get startled, but she still wanted to greet all the people who came to the office. When she was at the office, there were more rules to learn. She was not allowed to beg from staff if they were eating at their desks, and she could not go into the kitchen area where everyone prepared their lunch.

Sophie became so much a part of the office, especially when we ordered out for food once a week for a staff meeting

Sophie waiting for office guests

in the conference room. When the food order request form was being circulated to staff for everyone to choose their lunch item, there was always a line marked "Sophie." Sophie enjoyed hot dogs, hamburgers, chicken McNuggets, and sausage breakfast sandwiches. I am sure all of this fast food was not the greatest thing for her, but she became so much a part of the office staff that she always had a little treat when everyone else was eating lunch. In that way, she had her own snack, and never asked for food while the staff was eating at the conference room table.

In addition to the office, Sophie went many other places in her life. I previously mentioned the week she went on vacation with Lizzy, and we called it "Lizzy and Sophie's vacation." When we were invited to a friend's house out of town, Sophie and Lizzy were invited as well. They adjusted to overnight stays and were on their best behavior in a strange house.

Waiting for office guests in the later years

There were times when Sophie had to stay home, and when she did, she was always happy to see us return. When I came home from work, Sophie was always there to greet me. Somehow she knew I was coming and her head would be in the front window watching me pull into the garage. Whether I was early, on time or late, she was always in the window. I assume she knew when I was coming by hearing the garage door open. But maybe she looked out the window for a much longer period of time waiting for me to arrive.

Whether my wife or I came home first, we played the game "let's see." Sophie would greet us at the laundry room door, wagging her tail and barking. We would say "let's see" at the laundry room door. We then went into the rooms Sophie had access to and made sure she had not disturbed anything or had any sort of destructive behavior with anything in the room. For 99 percent of the time, there wasn't anything wrong; and Sophie would know and be excited about it. Sophie had an almost perfect record until she was twelve years old. She would run into the family room, circling around, and bark loudly looking for praise. We never gave her a treat, she just looked for praise.

If she did something wrong, which was very infrequent, her ears would be down when we came into the house. Sometimes, it would be a very minor misdeed, like pulling a paper or magazine off a table. It would not be damaged, but she knew she had done something wrong. We would ask her "who did this?" and send her to the laundry room as a time-out, just like a child. She anxiously waited until we released her, and then she came bounding toward us. In later years, when we asked "let's see?" she would go to the laundry room automatically without us asking if she had done anything wrong. As she lay in the laundry room looking out and pleading to be released, her expression said that she would do better next time.

Another trick we played with her was to take small dog biscuits, which we called cookies, and hide them somewhere in the family room. She got so good at finding them. We had to take her out of the room when we were hiding a dog biscuit in a different spot every day, making sure she could not see where we were putting it. We would put a cookie in the corner of the room, under the front window seat cushion, or on the fireplace hearth behind the basket. She then was invited back into the room to find it. Her sense of smell was extraordinary. She would enthusiastically sniff until she found it and then, with permission, was able to eat it. It never took her more than a minute or two to find it, and I do not recall a time when she wasn't able to find her treat.

As I mentioned, Sophie had a silly streak. One of the phases she went through as a young dog was eating cardboard. We thought it may have been some sort of vitamin deficiency, and asked the vet. But we were never able to figure out why. It started by her sticking her nose in my briefcase when it was left at home on the floor and no one else was home. She would then take a pad of writing paper out, tear off the back cardboard and eat it. She would not eat the paper itself. I would ask, "What happened to the cardboard?" and Sophie would pretend she had no idea.

She graduated from memo paper cardboard to Kleenex boxes. She would slightly tear the Kleenex box, remove all the tissue and set them aside on the floor, and then proceed to eat the cardboard Kleenex box. The worst thing she ate over the years was a cardboard box that contained a laser printer cartridge. She took the brand-new cartridge (wrapped in plastic) out of the box, set it aside, and proceeded to devour the box. If nothing else, it provided some entertainment, because the box was blue, and for the next two days Sophie's poop was multicolor blue. Fortunately, she never became sick from eating cardboard.

The ultimate Sophie trick was with a cardboard box filled with teacups and saucers. My wife's aunt had died, and her uncle gave my wife a collection of her fine china cups and saucers. As a child, my wife would visit her aunt and uncle, who had no children. Her aunt would play tea party with her, and use her expensive china. Over the years, her aunt collected many single beautiful cups and saucers, all of fine china. My wife brought them home and placed the box on the dining room floor. As you recall, the living room and the dining room of our house were off-limits to Lizzy and Sophie. This was enforced with a quick command and "no," and no specific gates were used for those rooms. The day after the box of teacups came to our house, "the girls" were home alone while my wife and I were at work. Apparently the old cardboard box the teacups were in was too much for Sophie to resist. We came home after being out for the day and noticed that the teacups were now visible in the dining room through the kitchen doorway. My wife immediately reacted to what damage could have been done to the china teacups. She walked into the dining room to see the cardboard box devoured, but the teacups were all perfectly fine; all had been removed from the box and placed on the carpeting. How Sophie gently took

Sophie and Anita share a birthday

them out of their wrappings and placed them on the floor without breaking any of the cups was unbelievable. While my wife was inspecting the cups, Sophie, of course, put herself in a time-out.

When Sophie was not at home, at the office, or at the hospital working, she would also visit nursing homes to see family and friends. Both my mother-in-law and mother spent the last years of their lives in a nursing home in Naperville, Illinois. Routinely, we took Sophie and Lizzy with us, and they would visit with other patients along the way. Sophie even became well-known in the nursing home, as she spent nine years going there on a regular basis, visiting her Nana, Grandma, or friend Anita.

One of Sophie's fun events she attended was a professional baseball game, at U.S. Cellular Field where the White Sox play. They had a dog day every year, for which we had to preregister. The dogs were allowed to parade onto the field before the game, and then go to their seat to watch the game. I don't know if Sophie was watching or not, but the White Sox won. I recorded the game on the DVR at home and replayed it the next day. Sophie made it on to the live telecast several times during the game, including the seventh inning stretch. Sophie thoroughly enjoyed the excitement and the extra attention from everyone around her.

Sophie's favorite activities were eating, riding in the car, and riding on our boat. When Sophie was about three years old, we bought a home on a lake in Southeastern Wisconsin. We did not want to stay too far away from our home due to our commitment of taking care of eighty-five-plus-year-old elderly parents. We also bought a pontoon boat to go out on the small, quiet, no-wake lake. The pontoon had a large flat platform that the dogs could wander about and look for long distances all around them. It became one of Sophie's favorite activities.

White Sox game at Cellular Field

Built in 1938, the house we bought was rather old, and we needed to do some basic remodeling. Some of the remodeling involved common-sense items that had to be replaced. Some of the remodeling was done for the benefit of the dogs. Most people would not have gone to the extent we did to make the house dog friendly. We always treated the dogs as part of our family. One of the first things we did to our lake house was to take out the back door and the storm door, and replace them with a storm door that was glass, top to bottom. In that way, the dogs looked out the door in the backyard, and could watch us work outside if they wanted to. I have many fond memories of the two of them lying down next to each other looking out the backyard watching us while waiting for us to come in.

Waiting for the Great Pumpkin

Sophie enjoyed the boat shortly after we bought it and learned to like it more every year. The boat was delivered to the public launch area across the lake from our house. My wife then had to drive the boat to our house across the lake. Sophie and I were waiting on the pier for her return. When my wife and the boat were several hundred feet off the pier, she saw Sophie and started to call to her. Sophie ran down the pier at full speed, heading toward her right off the pier into the water. I am not sure who was more afraid, the collie in the water, or me trying to get her out of the water, while I could not swim.

Collies typically do not like water and are very poor swimmers, due to getting their heavy coat waterlogged. In the first *Lassie* movie, Pal got the job to play Lassie because he was the only collie tested who would swim across the river. In 1941, Pal, who was a rescue dog from a pound, was being paid $5,000

Smiling on a boat ride

a week to be on the movie lot. This would be the equivalent of over $50,000 a week in today's dollars. Obviously, there is nothing wrong with being a celebrity dog. Sophie had no swimming ability and was not about to become Lassie. She remembered that day very well and was cautious while getting onto the boat in future years.

Sharing a boat ride with a friend

Sophie enjoyed sticking her head through the frame of the front door of the boat and acting as a masthead as we drove around. She enjoyed the wind in her face and her fur flowing back.

Sophie enjoyed the boat almost to the last days of her life. The month before she died, we brought her back to the lake and took her for what would be her last boat ride. The only difference was that Sophie came onto the boat at the public handicapped boat ramp. She could no longer do the thirty-two stairs to the bottom of the pier where the boat was parked at our house. She walked from the handicapped ramp to the platform of the pontoon as a proud senior dog. She enjoyed that last day almost as much as she enjoyed every day on the boat.

Sophie knew how to work, but she also knew how to have fun. How important it is to separate the two in our human lives, to know when we work to allow ourselves a time to play. As my elderly father-in-law used to say, "Enjoy yourself, it's later than you think." He was right, time passes by too quickly.

CHAPTER 7

Sophie Becomes a Celebrity

Sophie averaged three daily walks through the neighborhood on Monday through Friday and two on Saturday and Sunday. During her walks, Sophie was extremely observant and was always looking for people to greet.

The neighbors started to notice her daily routine. After doing this for many years, Sophie at six, seven, and eight years old was recognized by more and more people. Many people came to know Sophie by name, but I remained "the man who took Sophie for her walks." Our dog walker took Sophie for her half-hour, midday walk as well. Because of that, there were many instances when a person would walk up to me in the evening and say hello to Sophie. They had no idea who I was, but they knew Sophie from meeting her at her midday walk and wanted to greet her on her nighttime walk as well.

Sophie had strict rules she obeyed while walking. She would heel without a leash and stop and sit at curbs. At a young age, I taught her to stop, sit, and look both ways before crossing streets. If she ever got loose, which she didn't, I wanted to make sure that she looked before crossing the street. It was like taking a four- or five-year-old child for a walk. Even though she could not talk, her expressions and mannerisms showed that she enjoyed herself. She even enjoyed walks in the cold winter months, especially in the snow.

Another way Sophie gained fame was when we were asked to help spread the word about the animal assisted therapy program. When Sophie was age four, we were asked to do a community presentation at a middle school, to talk about volunteering and the hospital program in general to young children. The hospital volunteer coordinator asked Sophie and me to do it, and she and I volunteered, not knowing how long or detailed it was going to be.

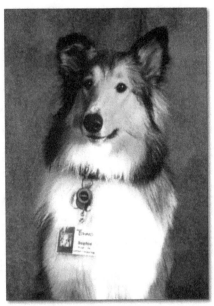

Official hospital portrait

We had no idea what was about to happen to us. We thought it was going to be a five- to ten-minute talk, and had not practiced anything and had nothing formally prepared. As I was about to learn, Sophie was a lot better at improvising than I could imagine.

I wore my blue hospital coat, and Sophie wore her hospital identity tag, and we went to the middle school for their fifth, sixth, and seventh period classes.

Upon entering the school, I was told by the school liaison that we were going to have the opportunity to teach the entire fourth, fifth, and sixth periods of various classes in the gym. So a lot of students and teachers would learn about the program. My jaw dropped, wondering what in the world could Sophie and I do for a forty-minute period to keep a bunch of middle schoolers entertained. Not only just once, but three times!

Each period was attended by over one hundred students in the school gymnasium. Have no fear, as Sophie was there. At the start of the period, I began by talking for five or ten minutes about the program at the hospital and why we did what we did, plus why a special dog was needed. Sophie sat and stayed obediently at my side. I moved around a little on the stage, but she did not move and instead watched me intently. I could tell that most of the kids were focusing on Sophie and not me. I then opened it up for discussion to the audience for questions.

I had brought with me a bunch of two-dollar bills (an old salesman's trick), which I had used in a sales presentation many years prior. I asked questions and then asked the audience for answers. The students were somewhat reluctant to answer the first couple questions. When a student answered a question successfully, they received a two-dollar bill from me and an invitation to come down to meet Sophie in person. The bills were hard for me to find and quite a novelty for the kids. I suddenly had many more students that were willing to participate. After the first two questions, I had twenty hands in the audience shooting up at once, competing to win the two dollars and to come down and greet Sophie.

Sophie was always happy and gracious to meet her new friends. So over the class period, she was introduced to at least twenty new friends. Sophie was the center of attention and thought everyone in the room had come to see her. She was right!

As part of the presentation, we wanted to duplicate the hospital environment. We had a student sitting in a folding chair or lying down in the two chairs as if in a hospital bed, and Sophie and I interacted with them as if we just entered their room in the hospital. I told the students to lie still until we approached them. As Sophie and I came up to the imaginary hospital bed, I then told them to either act happy, sad, grumpy, lonely, etc. It was a "virtual visit." I don't know who enjoyed it the most, Sophie or the kids.

The time flew by, and we only had time for three or four student-patient visits. We reenacted a complete visit at the hospital, and the kids and Sophie played off each other. At the end of the class, I asked for two volunteers and offered to teach the kids several secret hand signals to see if Sophie would respond to them. I had not done this before, nor practiced it, nor even knew whether Sophie would respond to a child giving her a command with a hand signal. We selected two kids to come down on the floor at once. The two kids spent a minute or two petting Sophie and getting to know her. As usual, Sophie bonded with both of them as if she had known them forever. We were now ready to amaze our audience.

I took one of the students to the opposite side of the gym over a hundred feet away and made Sophie sit and stay and had the student stand in front of her. I told the students to do whatever they could do to not let Sophie see me giving the secret signals to the other student across the room. Without either of the students' knowledge, I gave Sophie the "watch me" command and walked back to the other side of the room. I took the student not guarding Sophie and proceeded to give them a short course in hand signals I had made up over the years, teaching them five different hand signals. The hand signals were unique to Sophie and me, so no one could know about these signals even if they had a dog and trained them according to the books, because Sophie and I had made them up together. As I was showing the students hand signals without Sophie seeing, the other student was in the corner blocking Sophie's view. Of course, having given Sophie the "watch me" command, she kept leaning and straining each way around the student to see what I was doing, without getting up from her stay. I told the students "you can't let her see us," and it became quite entertaining to see the student moving around and trying to block Sophie's full view as Sophie kept straining to see me. It was all planned, although it was not practiced. We could not have rehearsed it better.

Now came the final test to see if the student who stood by me across the room could call Sophie back to them with a hand signal, without a voice command, and have Sophie sit in front of them. Sophie would then do the three or four other commands that I had showed the student based on the student's hand signal and not mine. It was quite an amazing performance where Sophie reacted beautifully. Fourth period quickly ended, and we had two more periods to go. By the time we got to periods five and six, Sophie and I had developed quite a well-rehearsed routine. She watched me and knew what I was going to do before asking her. That made it an even better performance. She had responded perfectly to three different students as she was taught, and listened to a student the same as if I had given the command myself.

The middle school presentation was very successful, and somehow made the local newspaper. Sophie was the talk of the town. Her story also appeared in other local newspapers or magazines over the years, including a publication called the *Collie Nose*. It was the story of special collies that have been adopted and gone on to do special things, including animal assisted therapy.

COLLIE RESCUE
OF GREATER ILLINOIS

The Collie Nose

Volume 3, Issue 1, March 2014

PET ASSISTED THERAPY - IT'S HISTORY AND VALUE

By Dale Mohr

Animal-assisted therapy (AAT) has its roots in ancient beliefs in the supernatural powers of animals and animal spirits that were first recorded in early hunter gatherer societies. Today it is recognized and accepted as a legitimate treatment, using animals to improve a patient's social, emotional, or cognitive functioning.

Therapy with animals began in the 9th century in Gheel, Belgium, teaching people with disabilities to care for farm animals as a form of rehabilitation program. Today animals used in therapy include domesticated pets, farm animals and marine mammals.

In the late 18th century at the York Retreat in England, led by William Tuke, the use of animals in treatment of the mentally ill was first reported. Later in the 1930's Sigmund Freud, who kept many dogs and often had his Chow-chow present during his pioneering sessions of psychoanalysis, noticed that the presence of the dog was helpful because his patients would find their speech or gestures would not disturb the dog. This reassurance encouraged them to relax and confide with the therapist.

Dr. Boris Levinson in 1961 in New York incorporated dogs in his therapy protocol for young people after he happened to leave his dog alone with a difficult child he was treating, and found the child talking to the dog when he returned.

More recently, experimental studies have attempted to gather better data to formally confirm these earlier findings. A study in 1984 by Dr. Wilson states that man's interest in animals is related to early human survival being partly dependent on the protective defensives early man observed in animals. Wilson's hypothesis suggests that we humans have an ingrained sense to recognize the assurance of safety, security and feelings of well-being when seeing animals in a peaceful state. A therapist with a pet can often trigger a change in the patient, making healing not only possible but faster.

Many nursing homes and hospitals began to elicit the help of cats and dogs as comfort for patients in times of need. The patients report elevated moods and a sense of comfort when the animal was around for only a few minutes. Additionally, the use of dogs seemed to create a more positive environment for the overall medical facility, reflected in reduced stress levels in the healthcare professionals. These findings were reported in a study by Cole in 2007 conducted over a three-month period.

D.A.Marcus et al in 2012 conducted a study to determine the benefits of using therapy dogs in an outpatient pain management clinic. Over a two month period patients were seated in a waiting room with a therapy dog. The patients visited by the therapy dogs were found to have a reduction in their pain rating and an improvement in their mood.

In order to become AAT or Pet Assisted Therapy (PAT) certified, a pet owner or therapist must go through the Pet Partners, formerly Delta Society, program that promotes the use of animals in therapy.

There is a four-step process to become a registered Pet Partners Team member. First step is training the dog handler to guide the animal in therapy sessions. They learn the signs in patients that signal comfort and acceptance. Second step is to have the dog screened and approved by a licensed veterinarian for any medical condition that might inhibit its use. In the third step the dog and handler are tested to check the skills and ability to react in therapy sessions. Finally, a Registration Application is submitted for approval by Pet Partners that the dog and owner are certified to assist in therapy in hospitals, retirement homes, prisons, schools for the handicapped, and the home.

As an example of the success of PAT, Edward Hospital in Naperville began the PAT program in 2002. To start, 15 teams were trained. Patients chose to have a dog visit during their hospital stay. In an interview with the Daily Herald (3/2/2012) Hospital President and CEO Pam Davis stated she "couldn't imagine any of our dogs being suited for an Animal-Assisted Therapy program at first."

Ten years ago, I was unaware of the rigorous training that would prepare every handler and dog for the highly selective program. Yet I defended the new program, cognizant of the connections animals can make with improving care of patients, especially adolescents. On ... the 10th anniversary celebration of the Animal-Assisted Therapy program (2012)... I could see dozens of tail-wagging pooches and their handlers greeting onlookers with cameras. Not a gentle yelp was heard as breeds ranging from a 3.5-pound Yorkshire terrier to a 172-pound mastiff were grouped together."

Davis praised Patty Kaplan, director of the Animal-Assisted Therapy program, and all the trainers and handlers who had developed "the favorite program at Edward." Today, 83 dog-and-handler teams participate and another 13 teams recently passed temperament training.

A CRGI adopter, Ted Slupik, has his own story about his collie, Sophie. She came to her owners as a "REJECT" via Lamb's Farm in 2001. Ted considers it very fortunate he adopted Sophie at 8 weeks of age. She is a people "person" and takes great pleasure in meeting new people, making her job as a therapy dog at Edward Hospital such a perfect fit. She "introduces" herself not only patients but to the patient's visitors, one at a time. In January 2014 she completed 11 years of service and continues as the longest serving therapy dog in the Edward Hospital program. Sophie is on call at all times.

Once, while visiting his mother-in-law who is an Alzheimer's patient at a care facility, Ted and Sophie came upon Leo, sitting in a wheel chair. Although normally unresponsive, Leo began to pat his leg, trying to get Sophie's attention. He also began calling her, saying "here girl" which was amazing as Leo had not spoken a word during the previous six months as a patient.

Sophie is part of many such stories and has been making a difference to those in need of comfort for over 12 years. From reject at Lamb's to compassionate therapy dog, she continues to enrich the lives of everyone she meets!

Thanks again to Dale Mohr

for this informative article.

Collie Humor

TRY GETTING THAT KIND OF INFORMATION ON THE INTERNET.

Another of Sophie's favorite activities was birthdays. She enjoyed birthdays, whether at home or other people's homes. For each of her birthdays, she was given a thick slice of meat, usually turkey. We also had candles and sang "Happy Birthday" to Sophie. For most of her birthdays, there were other family members or friends at her party. We would sing, and Sophie would smile in anticipation of her special treat.

The older she got, the more of an event it became. For each of her birthdays, we took her picture. My favorite picture of her is one with her celebrating her eleventh birthday at a nursing home she visited. She is smiling and all of her candles were lit,

Sophie's tenth birthday!

with my mother and Anita, an elderly friend who shared the date of Sophie's birthday, sitting on either side of her.

Sophie's eleventh birthday with her canine friend, Pixie

On command I asked her to speak, and believe it or not, that "speak" blew out the candles. Coincidence? I think not. She also enjoyed a treat for herself when it was any of our other dogs' birthdays. I remember missing some of the other dogs' birthdays, but we never missed a birthday for Sophie. She celebrated all thirteen years of her life with birthday events.

Another fun activity that got Sophie's attention was walking throughout downtown Naperville and on the Riverwalk. At the time, the Riverwalk was only about a six-block-square area. We would do this almost every weekend in the summer. She learned and began to know more and more people on these walks. Sophie would wait outside the stores with me while my wife went into a store to shop. Although Naperville has since become a much more dog-friendly place during the last few years, at that time dogs were not allowed in most of the stores. We would stand out front of a store, and almost everyone coming in or going out (or just passing by) would want to meet Sophie and learn about her. Gail, who wrote the

Sophie's portrait

article about Sophie and was the editor of the *Collie Nose*, originally met us outside a Naperville store.

Her celebrity status continued to grow when we took Sophie for a portrait to be put in a local humane society calendar to raise funds for homeless shelter dogs. The picture was done by a professional photographer. Sophie's picture made the calendar and the photographer, Tom Testolin of Kramer Photography, took many pictures of her because she was so beautiful. We bought a few pictures but not her main portrait. Several years after the pictures were taken, and while driving home from work one day, I passed the studio. I looked in the front display window of the studio, and to my surprise, there was a giant framed 3' x 4' portrait of a collie. It was Sophie!

I was so sure that I went home and told my wife about the picture. She insisted it couldn't be Sophie and that it was just a coincidence. The next morning my wife and I stopped at the front window of the studio, and sure enough, there was Sophie's picture in the most prominent place in the window; larger than any of the people pictures in the front of the store. I eventually went in and talked to Tom, and found out he liked the picture so much he used it on a regular basis as advertising for his pet photography business. He had been taking it to various dog shows and putting it up with his other pet pictures. Sophie's picture was successfully recruiting quite a lot of business.

My sister Jan and her daughters had gone to a dog show in Arlington Heights shortly after I became aware of the picture. Jan called me when she got back from the show to say she saw a picture of a dog that looked exactly like Sophie. As it turns out, it *was* Sophie's picture that she saw. It was the booth that Kramer Photography had at the dog show she attended. Sophie's picture stayed prominently displayed in the front of the photography studio for a year and a half, more than any other picture before or after. Hundreds of people passed by daily.

After being on display for a year and a half, I went to see Tom and told him the story of Sophie, who was about eleven years old at the time. He was so impressed with her service for so many years that he gave me the picture and frame. It's a brilliant portrait of her full exuberance as a nine-year-old collie, although she looked much younger. Tom liked the picture so much that he made a duplicate copy of the one he gave to me for their front window and replaced the one I had taken, so the duplicate stayed up for another four or five months after I had acquired the original.

In another picture story, a friend of mine once took a picture of Sophie and Lizzy together and had the picture made into official U.S. postage stamps. So Sophie and Lizzy were sent via the mail on birthdays and other occasions over a period of time until we ran out of the one hundred stamps that were made.

Lizzy and Sophie official U.S. postage stamps

As Sophie's reputation became more and more famous, on occasion I would Google her name to see if any hits came up in a search. At one time, I found twelve to fifteen instances where Sophie was listed in an article or story found by Google. What an amazing feat for this special dog. My wife has an older cousin and friend of the family (Al) who was not very computer literate. He once asked us if we would show him some "stuff" about the internet and how to research things and look them up. He was surprised and amused by reading some stories about Sophie on the internet that we "Googled." He then asked me to research his name. Al was seventy years old, had been in the military and had a successful career, and unbelievably, his name did not come up once in a search. Kind of makes it hard to believe that a dog could have twelve to fifteen hits on the Google search engine, and a human who lived seventy years had none.

Part of Sophie's special relationships was visiting my mother-in-law (Nana) and my mother (Grandma) when they were both in a nursing home, of which two years were concurrent with each other. Sophie had a close relationship with both of them prior to them being in the nursing home. They lived to be ninety-four and ninety-five years old respectively. Collies have a special way of looking at you when you speak, tilting their head from side to side and looking into your eyes as if they understand everything you are saying. Maybe Sophie understood more than I ever thought. Sophie had a special relationship with Nana, who would talk to her for a half-hour at a time.

We had an annual event at our home where Nana's five brothers and sisters would come and stay with us for a few days to have a family reunion. Most of her siblings lived out of town, and they came to stay with us once a year. They all enjoyed themselves and Sophie enjoyed the constant attention of the older crowd. After every occasion that the brothers and sisters would get together, as they left, they cried and hugged each other and said that this might be the last time they saw each other. How special it was for them to be able to celebrate as a family into their seventies and eighties and to have Sophie be an integral part of it, taking turns sitting at an older person's side. And how special it was for Sophie to sit and talk to my mother-in-law, Nana, and sit and watch all the other people talk. Sophie was everyone's best friend.

When Sophie sat next to you, she made it seem that she had been your dog for many years, and you knew her and she knew you. This was so even though Sophie had only met you shortly before. I do believe Sophie remembered the annual reunion event from year to year, and was their host and guardian for their three-day weekend for eight years, most of these times at Nana's side. Nana told many stories of growing up in the city of Chicago where there were always many dogs around and how she enjoyed them. Sophie and Nana retained a special relationship until Nana died when Sophie was eleven.

Sophie listening intently to her Nana while Nana's siblings are visiting

Showing that you can find celebrity status anywhere, even in a hospital, the following story occurred while doing the most unorthodox thing. One of the requirements of the hospital program was to be sure that your pet stayed healthy. The last thing you would want to do was to have a sick dog infecting a patient. I don't think a dog can give people a cold or any other disease, as only we humans can do to them, but safety was very important to the hospital.

Part of the hospital procedure to maintain your status in the program was to require the dog to have a six-month fecal test for parasites. The hospital sent out a kit which consisted of two vials, half-filled with liquids, put in a large plastic bag. After the test, the samples were required to be dropped off at the hospital laboratory (in a clear plastic bag with large "Biohazard" orange letters on it). If you saw the bag, the color and markings of it, you would probably stay away for fear of contamination. Sophie was required to produce twenty-plus samples during her therapy years at the hospital. The laboratory of the hospital that took these samples was in a remote part of the hospital in the basement. I would usually hand out one of Sophie's "business cards" with the sample and tell them about Sophie. Over the years, the people who took the sample at the lab downstairs would ask about Sophie and got to know her, even though she was not allowed to go down into the basement herself. When the lab technicians saw her name on the bag, many of them knew or had heard of Sophie.

One weekday morning before work, I was taking in the sample before 6:30 a.m. and I was in quite a hurry. I usually put the biohazard bag in another bag so no one could see it, but on this day I had the biohazard bag by itself, without its usual camouflage cover-up bag. A woman walked up to me as I entered the hospital that happened to be an employee and nurse and recognized the bag. She asked if I had a dog in the animal assisted therapy (AAT) program, to which I responded yes. She then asked me what type of dog it was, and I replied that it was a collie. Without missing a beat, the woman asked me if the dog was named Sophie. She had never met Sophie, but had heard about her from other nurses and patients on different floors at the hospital and about some of Sophie's extraordinary visits. She then volunteered to take our sample down to the lab because she knew it was Sophie's. How is that for celebrity valet service? How could she care so much about Sophie, a dog that she never met, that she was willing to carry down the "biohazard bag" based on her secondhand knowledge of the dog? Coincidence? I think not.

Another place Sophie visited was the wake for the husband of a fellow handler at the hospital. The deceased's wife, Barb, was the primary handler of a thirteen-year-old dachshund therapy dog named Lumpi. The couple were both in their seventies. Since they were both dog lovers, dogs were invited to attend the wake. Barb and Lumpi had enrolled in the Animal Assisted Therapy program about nine months after Sophie and I started, and she was part of the second-longest-serving handler and dog team at the hospital. Sophie and I were the longest-serving team at the hospital, and our record is still intact today. I think we had a little bit of a rivalry, because Barb would often ask me how much longer I intended to volunteer with Sophie. I really think she wanted to be the team with the longest-serving record.

We arrived at the wake for her husband, and it was very well attended. There was a line through the church, out the door, and down the sidewalk to come by and pay one's respects. The line could have easily been one hundred people. So here was Sophie at my side, slowly moving up the line to enter the church where the memorial service was being held, waiting our turn. Sophie took in all the people around her and behaved perfectly. She gently and quietly interacted with whoever greeted us or petted her. Sophie knew that this was a solemn time and acted appropriately.

Several of the people came up to us and said, "Is this Sophie?" I told them that it was. I asked them how they knew about Sophie. As it turns out, Barb and Lumpi the Dachshund had told many of her friends that Sophie the Collie was the only dog at the hospital in the program with a longer term of service than her dog. It must have meant a lot to her if three or four people came up to us and knew Sophie, having never met her. Unfortunately, shortly thereafter, Lumpi could not continue to visit at the hospital due to health issues, and Sophie continued to add to the record, which I do not believe will ever be broken by another dog.

As we were leaving the church, Sophie was still on high alert based on the hundreds of people around and being in different and strange surroundings. Sophie noticed a young man in the corner of the church all by himself. For as obedient as Sophie always was, she was not going to leave the church without seeing this young man. The young man seemed out of place: anxious and lonely. As we approached him, the man reached out and anxiously started to pet her, a little harder than normal. As it turns out, the young man was the son of the man who had died and Barb. He also appeared developmentally disabled. How lonely to be by yourself with your father deceased, and hundreds of people around, scared, but with no one to talk to. Sophie knew from across the room of his torment and went over to comfort him as only she could. I had brought Sophie to the event, and once again she shined in the moment based on her abilities and instincts. Sophie picked the neediest person out of the crowd and went to help him. If only we could know who needs our assistance and be as quick and willing to help as Sophie was.

Sophie even got recognition from one of our town's policemen. Sophie was riding with my wife while she was coming to the office to pick me up. She was running late. As a result, she was speeding through town and a police officer stopped her. The officer took her license to his car to check and came back to her car with his ticket pad, preparing to write a ticket. At that time, my wife rolled down the back car window and out popped Sophie. The policeman went on to explain that as a kid, his grandmother had a collie, and "what a great dog she was!" Of course Sophie became immediate friends with the police officer. My wife came away with a warning and no ticket, thanks to Sophie.

CHAPTER 8

Sophie's Special Powers

No doubt about it, Sophie was a very intelligent dog. I taught her many of the things she did. But I would say that most of the special things she did were learned on her own through instinct and life experiences, which makes them even more amazing. This chapter is a summary of some of the uniquely extraordinary things she did.

Sophie was much more a child socializing with adults than a dog being a loyal pet. As I mentioned before, when she first passed away, I started to remember many of the things Sophie did that affected so many people's lives. Some of the events are just simply unexplainable. After Sophie passed away, I spent the next month writing down two or three sentences about different events in Sophie's life. I began to tell some of the stories to family and friends, who said it sounded like episodes from *Lassie.* I remarked that there was only one difference: all of my stories were true.

As our Chihuahua, Lizzy, got older (age fifteen or sixteen), she began to have some new health problems. Although her major orthopedic health problems happened at age nine, and we had overcome most of them, she started to slow down and have other issues at age fifteen. One of the issues was for a brief period of time, and still uncertain of its cause, Lizzy had incurred several mild, short-term seizures. The first seizure that we knew of was at home with Sophie in one room, Lizzy in another, and my wife and me in a third. Lizzy started to have a seizure, and Sophie must have sensed it. Sophie came to find the two of us, barked until we followed her and took us to Lizzy. It was almost as if she was pulling our sleeve to come and help Lizzy. By her actions, Sophie had told us Lizzy was in distress and needed our help. I held Lizzy in my lap and after a minute saw her calm down, and the seizure soon passed.

The second episode of Lizzy having a seizure occurred several weeks later. Sophie came and alerted us prior to the seizure even starting. Sophie wanted us to follow her and took us to sit by Lizzy. We sat quietly, not knowing why Sophie had done this. After a minute or two, Lizzy started to have another seizure. This time we were right there to comfort her and hold her from the start, and it lasted less than a minute. This was Lizzy's second and last seizure. We were never able to determine the cause. I know you can train service dogs to sense seizures in people prior to them happening, but Sophie was never formally taught to recognize seizures. It was somehow instinctive to her, not only that Lizzy was in discomfort, but for Sophie to have thoughts where actions are required to find a solution.

In addition to her hospital work, Sophie would visit friends and family either in the hospital or at a nursing home where my mother-in-law (Nana) and my mother (Grandma) resided. Nana was at the nursing home for five years after her husband passed away. Initially she was there just for assisted living help, but the death of her spouse accelerated her Alzheimer's disease, and she was moved to a special floor. The third floor of the nursing home was reserved for Alzheimer's patients and other patients who had difficulty communicating with others. Many of the more severe patients were not able to communicate at all.

For almost four years, my wife and I would go to visit Nana several times a week. We would usually take Sophie with us and walk through the activity room on the Alzheimer's floor and greet all the patients who were sitting in there. This nursing home made it a policy to get all the patients out of their rooms every day, to help them socialize and communicate, even if they did not want to. Many of the patients never had any visitors. Sophie would introduce herself to a patient and stand and wait until she was acknowledged before moving on to the next patient. Sophie was able to provoke a response (pet, smile, and laugh), even from patients who did not normally interreact with staff or others.

An unusual event happened as we were walking Sophie through the activity room while the patients were watching television. A man in a wheelchair was sitting in a far corner. He made eye contact with Sophie and began to pat his leg and said "here girl" to call her to him. Sophie noticed him and slowly started to walk toward him. He continued calling "here girl" until Sophie got close enough and sat down next to him so that he could pet her. This man, named Leo, asked, "Dog name?" We told him "Sophie." He spoke in broken sentences for a brief time and seemed to really enjoy the visit. Sophie intently watched and listened to Leo as he spoke very softly. She continued to nudge him until he responded back.

After we were done visiting all of the patients in the activity room, we left to go down the hall to visit with Nana in her room, which was at the far end of the hallway. Upon exiting the activity room, you were required to pass the nurses' station for the floor. There was a couple standing and talking to the charge nurse. They were crying. I asked whether there was anything we could do to help. The woman answered, "No, you've already done something." Asking what she meant, she explained that Leo, the man in the wheelchair, was her father. He had been at the nursing facility on the Alzheimer's care floor for almost six months. *Today was the first day he spoke!*

What I thought was tears of sorrow were actually tears of joy. Whatever the brief encounter with Sophie did to remind him of something a long time ago, or to get him to speak, was a wonderful thing. We had thought someone had died when we first saw the couple at the nurses' station, and it turned out to be a very happy moment for Leo and his family. Although he never became a great conversationalist during his remaining time at the nursing home, Leo was able to speak and at least respond to nurses if he needed some type of help or if he was in pain. It was amazing how I went from assuming the worst and being sad to experiencing a moment of joy, delivered by Sophie.

We would see Leo many other times. It was almost as if he knew we were coming because we always seemed to find him waiting by the elevator to welcome Sophie. Another time we saw him after our first visit, my wife asked him if he would like to give Sophie a "cookie" (our word for dog biscuit). He nodded his head enthusiastically and my wife gave Leo a Milk-Bone, but apparently something got lost in the translation. That day Leo had a Milk-Bone for his dessert. Leo thought it was *his* cookie.

Another thing Leo would do when he first saw Sophie get off the elevator, was to follow her down the hall in his wheelchair, peddling with his feet as fast as he could to keep up with or catch Sophie. This type of exercise was exactly what the nurses tried to get Leo to do many times on his own. He was always willing to do it to see Sophie for a longer period of time and got his exercise this way twice a week. Leo never learned my name or my wife's name, but he certainly remembered Sophie every time we came to visit. Leo lived several more years, and we have Sophie to thank for giving him back the ability to communicate.

After Lizzy passed away at age sixteen and a half, Sophie became very lonely without her lifelong companion. It was as if every day she waited to see Lizzy come home. They had been the closest of companions for eight years. Their size difference didn't matter. Sophie always looked out for Lizzy and protected her from any harm. Months passed, and based on her slow and deliberate demeanor, Sophie surely missed Lizzy and mourned the loss of her friend. At that point in time, we decided to pursue getting another dog to be a companion for Sophie. We wanted a smaller dog, but one not quite as fragile as Lizzy the Chihuahua was.

We came upon Forrest, a man who raised champion papillons, the breed trade name being called Zelicaon Papillons, meaning looking like black butterflies. He normally sold dogs only to breeders, but in this case he made an exception as he had a young, undersized female so small that he would not be able to breed or sell her. That's how Pixie came about.

Forrest's farm was located about two hundred miles west of Chicago. We made a day trip on a very busy Saturday to see the dog. Forrest was going to hold her for us, as he knew of my interest in therapy dogs. We brought Sophie out of the car to be introduced to Pixie; and just as Sophie had been submissive to Lizzy at their first meeting, Pixie was submissive to Sophie. However, this was a big dog with a little puppy, not a big puppy (like the ten pounds that Sophie was with Lizzy). Sophie was never aggressive, and I just thought she always thought of Pixie as a friend of Lizzy. Pixie was slightly bigger, same coloring, slightly sturdier, and a little bit more aggressive than Lizzy. Pixie ultimately grew to six pounds, whereas the breed standard for a female papillon was eight to ten pounds. So "Pixie" was a breeder's reject, just as Sophie was.

As a puppy, whenever Pixie would do something that was not right, Sophie would correct her. Sophie was potty trained in one day, as incredible as it sounds. Pixie, on the other hand, took three months. In the beginning, Pixie was very afraid

Puppy Pixie sleeping next to Sophie

and timid. She was the runt of a litter of six puppies and was pushed around by her five male siblings. Sophie watched out for Pixie, took away her fears, and gave her the confidence that she has today.

There were a lot of things that Pixie did because Sophie was around to teach her, knowing the boundaries of the rooms that dogs were allowed in, where they ate, and where they slept. Sophie was there as the enforcer of all the rules, and some of those rules went by the wayside after Sophie passed away. As it turns out, Pixie never jumped onto the furniture when Sophie was around. What we thought was our good training of Pixie was Sophie monitoring and enforcing the rules.

The first six months that Pixie was with us, she was a very active puppy, and you could tell that it sometimes annoyed Sophie.

Pixie steals Sophie's bone

Sophie still tolerated everything Pixie did to her, including stealing Sophie's food and her bones, so once again you had a small six-pound dog taking food and bones away from a sixty-five-pound dog without a challenge.

Pixie was five months old when she came to her forever home with us. Since training did not start at eight weeks for her, she was more difficult to train and had some bad habits that she had learned in her first five months. We bought a small crate for Pixie, which she stayed in during the day if no one was home. We kept her in the crate for about three months and were uncertain how long it would be necessary. The crate had a door, that required lifting up a rod and turning it to open the door and it was challenging to operate. One day, we came home and saw Pixie was on the loose. We thought that one of us had failed to lock the crate. This went on for four consecutive days, where Pixie was loose every day that we came home. We finally figured out that Sophie determined that she wanted Pixie loose with her and would open the crate door daily after we left for work. How Sophie was able to lift and turn the rod to release Pixie, we don't know, as it was not an easy task.

By this time Pixie had grown up, and acted fine being free, as long as Sophie was there to supervise. Sophie seemed happy again to have a companion, who looked up to her, and they became almost as good friends as Lizzy and Sophie were.

Pixie was an escape artist her first year and required a leash until she was almost five. Sophie, on the other hand, was at my side without a leash from six months on and would never run away. Pixie was a very fast little dog that you could never chase down or catch. Running was a game with Pixie. She would let you get close to her, reach down to grab her, and off she would go again.

One night in the middle of winter while Pixie was still very young, I came home about 7:00 p.m. It was dark, cold, and snowing. Only Sophie and Pixie were home. I entered the garage, walked into the laundry room and hit the button to close the overhead garage door. Normally, I closed the garage overhead door before entering the laundry room. Pixie was waiting at the laundry room door. She saw the opening in the garage door and ran out full speed, before I was able to catch her.

I threw on my coat and ran out the laundry room, calling for Pixie. It was below freezing, pitch-black, and the snow continued. If Pixie wound up being lost outside in these conditions, I don't think she could have survived for a very long period of time. No one was around in the neighborhood or at home to help me, and after about fifteen minutes of searching, I came back home to get the car and started driving around in wider and wider circles to the adjacent streets. As I got closer to the house, on the other side of the street, I noticed Sophie herding Pixie back to the house. I watched Sophie get to the house, and she put Pixie in the corner of the open garage and did not let her leave there. At that point, Sophie stood at the entrance to the garage and started barking to call me. Sophie blocked any attempt of Pixie's to leave the garage.

Unbeknownst to me after I ran out of the house, I had left the laundry room door ajar, which Sophie proceeded to open and go out and find Pixie. Where the two dogs were for fifteen minutes, I have no idea. But somehow Sophie went to find Pixie on that dark, cloudy and snowy day and brought her back to safety. I know collies are herding dogs, but for Sophie to go out and find Pixie and bring her back on her own, with no instruction or command from me, was remarkable. She did it based on instinct and her critical thinking ability. Anytime Pixie started to bother or annoy Sophie, I kiddingly often reminded Sophie that her rescue may have been her last chance to get rid of Pixie. But the two dogs developed a close bond.

One time, we took Sophie on a road trip to the cemetery to see my wife's father's grave. On the way there, my wife and I reminisced a lot about her father and some of his characteristics. He was a dog lover and he loved Sophie, as well as our two previous dogs. As we entered the cemetery gates, Sophie became extremely agitated. There had been a severe wind and rainstorm on the drive down, which had just subsided. Sophie was a very good car rider, so her anxiety and barking and crying and running back-and-forth in the back of the truck was alarming. We did not know what was wrong with her or what she was trying to tell us. Perhaps she was sick or needed to go outside. We drove near to where we thought the gravesite was, parked the truck and went around the back to calm Sophie down, asking her if she was okay.

While we stood at the back of the truck, petting and calming Sophie, a huge oak tree branch broke and fell down just a short distance in front of us. Had we been walking toward my father-in-law's grave, it most certainly would've hit us. Could Sophie have known something bad was going to happen, and delayed us for a few minutes from getting out of the car and taking that walk? A coincidence? I think not.

As I explained before, and through many other untold stories, there were hundreds of events in Sophie's life affecting others that could not have been coincidences. After the tree branch had fallen, Sophie became perfectly calm. We went about and visited my father-in-law's grave as if nothing had happened. We visited the cemetery numerous times after that with Sophie, and she never had another reaction to being there. As a matter of fact, when we let her out of the car, she would know exactly where the headstone was and find it on her own before we did. She was very proud to have found it, and we praised her for being so smart. Dogs can't read, but how a dog could pick out one headstone amongst hundreds, I cannot explain.

Another one of Sophie's extraordinary abilities related to communicating with people she barely knew. You could say almost anything and ask her to do it, and she would understand what you said. She also would sit and look at people, and let them talk and make them believe she understood every word.

My mother-in-law (Nana) was one of those people. Every time she saw Sophie, Nana would speak to Sophie at length. In her later years, with the onset of Alzheimer's, it became very difficult for Nana to communicate with anyone. Nana could no longer recognize me or her three children or any of her family. The one she remained able to recognize in her declining years and know by name was Sophie. Sophie brought a smile to Nana's face, and would nudge her until she received a reaction back and get her to talk until she could no longer verbalize.

One day, my wife received a call from the nursing home indicating her mother was having what appeared to be some severe pain issues and crying out on a recurring basis in the early hours of the morning. She was not able to communicate the problem with the staff. So the staff could not understand her or know how to treat her. The nurses at the nursing home had asked if my wife and I would come in and talk to Nana, and try to decipher what the problem was. As we walked into the room, we had Sophie with us as usual. Nana was very agitated that day and said some very mean things to my wife as we entered her room, of course not knowing what she was saying. As gentle and loving as Nana was most of her life, the opposite personality now overtook her as part of her disease. My wife began to cry. I told her to go out in the hall and take a break and let me see what I could do to help figure out what was going on.

As I talked to Nana, I held her hand, looked right at her and began to speak very slowly and deliberately. I kept asking her if she could tell me what was wrong with her, so we could help her. I repeated it several times so I thought she knew what I was asking, but she did not speak. She would shake her head "no," but was otherwise unable to communicate. She was listening to me but watching Sophie intently. Finally, as a last resort and as Sophie sat next to her and continued to nudge her hand during the conversation, I asked her if she would tell Sophie what was wrong. Without hesitation, she went on to talk to Sophie, at which time I was able to learn what the issues were. I would ask questions to her from Sophie, and she would respond. She would not talk to nurses, she would not talk to family, she would not talk to her own daughter, she would not talk to me, but she did talk to Sophie. I think all the conversations that Nana had with Sophie over the years were much more understood by Sophie than I ever realized.

Almost ten years ago, I incurred a significant leg injury. After six months of many specialized tests and treatments, it turns out the problem was undiagnosed severe shingles on my leg resulting in peripheral neuropathy. Although at least six different doctors examined me during the first six months, no one came up with the correct diagnosis. By then the damage had been done and could not be reversed. I would deal with the pain for nine more years, reduced by medication but never dissipated. Walking the dogs would sometimes help alleviate the pain, but the leg was so sensitive to cold temperatures that it would almost collapse in below-zero weather.

The day after Sophie left us, and after nine years of pain, the pain was gone. I asked my doctor and my neurologist about this. There was no reasonable medical explanation for it to be gone. My leg is still pain free, a year plus later.

The final story of this chapter relates to an incident with my wife Bernie. For a period of time, Bernie had some serious health issues, including what turned out to be a blood clot in her lung, which if left undetected could have broken loose and killed her.

One day I was out of the office, and called Bernie to tell her I would not make it back to the office that day. Bernie said she was feeling quite ill and dizzy and was going to go home. I asked her if she wanted to wait for me or have somebody else drive her, and she thought she could make it home herself.

So Bernie drove home, about a distance of six miles, put the car in the garage, and walked into the house. She had accidently left her cell phone in the car, and upon walking into the laundry room and then the bathroom off the garage, she collapsed on the bathroom floor. Bernie was passed out for what she thought was less than a minute when Sophie came over and began to lick her face. Sophie stood by her for a while, at which time my wife tried to stand up. She could not stand up and fell back to the floor again, unable to get up. At this point, Sophie left her side and went back into the family room. Sophie went to the table, picked up the portable phone from its cradle by its tip antenna, and brought it back to my wife. As a matter fact, Sophie let it go from her teeth as she was standing above Bernie, and it bonked her on her head.

Bernie was able to take the phone and call for help. How Sophie knew of the danger and picked up a phone and brought it back for help is unexplainable. Sophie had never touched the phone before, nor ever picked up the phone since that time. How could a dog have the intelligence to interpret the unique circumstance, know the immediate need of the situation, and be able to understand and help the situation by bringing a phone to Bernie?

Dogs are not supposed to be able to think in logical sequences and plan out their behavior accordingly. As smart as Sophie was, I don't think I could have ever taught her a trick of getting the phone and bringing it to me. How did that happen and what made it happen? Was it a miracle or a coincidence? We'll never know. It was another example of Sophie being the best she could be at helping another person in their life whenever she could. Bernie was able to call for emergency help and eventually fully recovered.

CHAPTER 9

The Later Years

As Sophie continued her therapy work, more and more people at the hospital came to know and remember us. They knew me by appearance; they knew Sophie by name. The staff, the doctors, and nurses would all want to stop and see Sophie and acknowledge her work with patients and visitors and looked forward even more to watching Sophie "doing her job." I am sure Sophie felt very good based on all the attention and acclamations she was receiving. You could see it in her eyes, smile, and prance. It was almost as if the people who knew her were greeting Sophie as a queen, her royal highness. This made Sophie feel wonderfully welcomed.

Each night before we went up to the patient rooms, we would stop at the concierge desk and ask whether there were any special requests to see a dog. Sometimes there were even special requests to see "Sophie, the Collie" based on other family members who were in the hospital knowing of Sophie. The concierge personnel were all volunteers who were there to help and guide people coming to see a patient and get them to the right place.

Sophie came to know a volunteer named Bernie, a lady originally from New Zealand, who was at the concierge desk on Friday nights. She was always anxious to greet Sophie and came out from around the counter to acknowledge her. Sophie would look for Bernie as we came through the turnstile door (not easy to navigate for a dog).

In the later years, I broke my own rule about Sophie with Bernie. Once a therapy dog is on duty, it is best not to give them any treats, and certainly none before working. A dog will begin to expect a treat from other patients, and start looking for them in every room instead of concentrating on their job of visiting. A therapy dog must work for recognition, not treats. I didn't want to distract Sophie from her job to visit and make people feel better, even if for only a little while. Bernie liked Sophie so much, and over the years she praised and petted and talked to her as if she were a child. Sophie returned the love and kindness she was shown.

Volunteer Bernie greeting Sophie

Bernie eventually brought in multiple boxes of dog treats to have on hand primarily for Sophie, but also for all of the therapy dogs. Sophie was even more anxious to get into the hospital and get a treat from Bernie. Not only to get a treat each time she went to the hospital, but to get a treat before even working, for doing nothing. I know Sophie enjoyed the spoiling of this event, and fortunately it did not change her behavior when visiting patients at the hospital. Bernie became a dear friend of Sophie and came to visit several times at our home. She was also an amateur photographer and took many beautiful pictures of Sophie.

Another group at the hospital that we saw on a regular basis were five young teenagers, around thirteen years old, who were practicing for their orchestra. There was a large open space in the lobby with a piano where visitors could congregate. The group volunteered and performed in this general lobby of the hospital on Fridays. The teenagers were all very talented children playing violin, cello, and piano on a regular basis for people at the hospital who were visiting or waiting outpatient therapy, or just visitors waiting to go to a patient's room. Sophie and I would take a break during our three hours of visits and listen to them play. Sophie seemed to enjoy their craft, especially if they played Mozart. The young group also enjoyed watching her sitting and intently listening to the music. At the end of playing a piece, they would talk to and pet Sophie. Sophie would smile and, if she could talk, probably would have said "Good job!"

Many times, Sophie was their only audience. The children were so talented, I could name a classical piece that they did not have music prepared for, and they would most times be able to play the piece, or at least the beginning part, from memory. What wonderful, dedicated kids, giving part of their time on a Friday night at such a young age to entertain people at a hospital, to make it not so bad for the people and patients that had to be there and to help pass the time they had to wait.

During our twelve-plus years at the hospital, the Animal Assisted Therapy program grew in popularity, and more and more dogs became part of the program. At one point, before Sophie retired from the program, there were up to eighty active dogs, with four or five dogs per shift per day to visit people seven days a week. Most of the volunteer visits were during the day. Friday nights were usually more crowded with visitors than any other night. There finally were enough dogs to cover the expanded needs of the hospital, which had almost doubled in size from the start to the end of Sophie's therapy work. We would never be able to visit all the floors of the hospital ourselves again, as we did in Sophie's first year. Fortunately, with the growth of the volunteers, we were never required to do so.

AAT Dog plaques, 109 members, 80 active

As a result of the expansion, the hospital dog coordinator decided that, in order to maintain quality, it was necessary to retest all the therapy dogs in the program every two years. The retest would consist of a group lesson of ten to fifteen dogs doing routine exercises and commands while the monitors watched. The dogs could not interact with any other dog during the testing. This was never a problem with Sophie, since she was always much more interested in people and not other dogs.

After the group exercises, the dogs were pulled out one by one for an individual test. This individual test, with an Animal Assisted Therapy Dog Tester Observer, could last anywhere from five to ten minutes, depending on the dog's ability. Sophie's first retest was at age seven. As we went around the room in circles and did the group exercises, I spent more time observing the other dogs to see whether they were behaving correctly, rather than watching Sophie. I knew she was extremely well behaved and would do all of the routine things perfectly. Sophie would amazingly know when another dog did something out of order as soon as I noticed it. Many of the other dogs were not so perfect. Sophie and I happened to be the first ones to be pulled out of the group to have an individual test.

After less than one minute with Sophie individually testing, the tester said we're obviously wasting both of our times here, as Sophie is just a super therapy dog. Her test had ended and she passed with flying colors. She was retested again at ages nine, eleven and thirteen. At ages nine and eleven she again was far and away the best in class. The testing at age eleven was difficult, as it was done outside in 95-degree heat, and it was very tough on her. That was the first time I looked at her and thought maybe I should not be putting her through this regimen and stress as she was getting older.

But every time I thought about retiring her, we would have a visit where Sophie would make such a difference in that person's well-being that we just had to endure and go on. The tester remarked how unbelievably good Sophie was, even at age eleven.

When Sophie was eleven, one of her friends, an eleven-year-old white West Highland terrier named Lilly, was retaking the test with us and failed. Lilly had been in the program for about seven years. Lilly's owner, Laurie, was shocked and devastated after failing the test and didn't know what to do. If a dog in the program failed their bi-annual update test, they were allowed one retest. Sophie and I asked if we could spend some time with Lilly and Laurie, going through the different trials of what was needed to pass, so Lilly could learn by watching Sophie. We spent a couple sessions of training in my backyard with emphasis based on the parts of the test that Lilly had failed, with Sophie leading the way. Lilly seemed to want to follow Sophie. Lilly was retested and passed with flying colors and stayed as part of our group until the very end.

At age thirteen, Sophie was summoned to be tested again. She had some difficulty getting up and down multiple times in a quick fashion because of her arthritis, but she made it through the test. We both knew this would be the last time she would be tested, and our days of therapy work would soon come to an end. Sophie would not be the best dog in the class this time due to her physical limitations. But she was still the smartest, best behaved, and most compassionate of the group. She would be great that way up until her last visit at the hospital.

The last year of Sophie's visits began her "farewell tour." During that time, my wife Bernie decided to follow along on a few occasions and watch us work. She took pictures of Sophie

Sophie with Lilly the dog, Laurie, and Ted at work

and me and her other Friday night friends in the volunteer room so we would remember how wonderful the experience was. As it turns out, all of our Friday regular group dogs eventually died or resigned right before Sophie did her last visit. So she was the longest-serving dog of our group, and she was longest-serving dog of the hospital program when she retired after twelve-plus years.

Bernie followed us through the various floors to watch Sophie in action. Although she certainly knew what pet therapy work was, she never realized how intense Sophie was at her job, making sure to greet and meet all people she encountered, and how her behavior was absolutely perfect in going into and out of rooms and knowing all the rules of the hospital. Sophie was still able to do a wonderful job at therapy work, she just could not do it for as long a period of time as she used to.

When doing our orthopedic ward visits, in some instances, Sophie would not have been in the room more than five feet, and the patient would ask, "Is that Sophie?" I then asked the patient how they knew it was Sophie, and they would respond that they had seen her three or four or five years earlier when they were having their other hip or knee operated on, or recalled her visiting another family member, yet they still remembered her by name as one out of eighty dogs. What an amazing impact Sophie must have had on these patients. Her previous encounter with a patient could have been as little as three minutes, six years ago, and the patient would recall the visit and Sophie's name. They had no idea I was the same handler and would ask, "Are you the same man who brought her before?"

As people get older, they get brasher and can say almost anything. I called it "old and bold." So most of the orthopedic patients were sixty-five and older and someone would ask, "Are you the same man who brought Sophie the last time? Because the person who brought her last time was much younger and thinner." I would chuckle and say yes, I was that person. I had changed a lot, but apparently Sophie had not. They did not know me but remembered Sophie as if they had met her yesterday. She made her presence known and touched these people in a permanent way that most people in their lives were not able to do.

The recognition of Sophie on a "second visit" did not happen once or twice, but hundreds of times. A coincidence? I think not. If you or I had met someone casually for a few minutes a year or two before and was introduced to them and told their name, there is a small chance that any of us would recall that name years later.

One of Sophie's physical problems in later life was her vision. It was not cataracts, but it was her losing her vision from the bottom up. This apparently is a common thing amongst older dogs. As a result, Sophie became reluctant to go down the stairs. Not because she couldn't do the stairs, but because she was not seeing out of the bottom 20 percent of her vision. At home, we began to carry her downstairs in the morning from our room to prevent any mishaps. Each night she still would be able to go up on her own, but she had fear of coming down, only because she could not see. She was a big and lanky dog to carry down, but we created a routine that she was very accepting of. My worry was getting caught in the hospital and having to use the stairs as an emergency exit if the elevators were out of operation. Fortunately, that never happened.

At home, Sophie maintained a routine she thought of on her own at age five. After waking up in the morning and going outside, she would come back upstairs and wait for me outside of the bathroom until I was showered and dressed and ready to come downstairs. She maintained that routine until she was almost eleven and stopped once it was more difficult to go down the stairs. Without missing a beat, Pixie took Sophie's place in coming upstairs and waiting for me once Sophie could not. How did Sophie communicate this and teach Pixie how to do this? I will never know, but Pixie assumed "this job" with the same dedication Sophie had.

Sophie also began to spend more and more time at work with me at my office. Mostly so I could keep her company; but also to give her a break from a new rambunctious puppy, Rosebud. Rosebud was a sable-and-white collie that we acquired when Sophie was twelve years old. I thought that collies were a smart breed and that all collies were as smart as Sophie. In the beginning, Sophie was anxious around Rosebud, so Sophie went to work with me two or three times a week.

Sophie had her own mat, bed, and drinking bowl in my office. Clients that came in to see me began to expect her to be there and were disappointed if she was not there. She became a celebrity with clients, even more so than at the hospital. She was in the conference room for many meetings and helped to create a relaxed atmosphere when important matters were discussed. Over the years, Sophie easily met three hundred different clients who considered her a friend. She greeted them enthusiastically, and they returned her happiness and affection right back.

Sophie and puppy, Rosebud

At age eleven, Sophie began to have trouble getting into and out of our Tahoe truck. The leap up or down was quite high and quite a strain. With hindsight, having her jump down out of the car onto concrete over the many years was probably a bad idea and contributed to her orthopedic issues. Rosebud, as a young puppy, had difficulty jumping up, so it must have been much harder for Sophie

Sophie watching out the office window

than I ever realized. We decided to look around and get a car that would be more accommodating to Sophie. As much as my wife and I said we would never drive a minivan, we bought a Dodge Caravan primarily to transport Sophie around. The middle and the back seats folded flat. The threshold of getting up and down was less than a foot, and it made it much easier to get into and out of that car for Sophie. She thoroughly enjoyed it, and she seemed to be much sturdier lower to the ground in her "new" car. She would still be able to look out the window and actually see more. That was Sophie's car, shared by Pixie and eventually shared by Rosebud, but Sophie "owned" the middle door and windows. Pixie rode shotgun on her bed on the console in the front seat and Rosebud rode in the far back of the van.

In her later years, Sophie usually came into the kitchen and barked to let us know that she was hungry. She would also diligently watch what was being prepared. Once, when we did not have much food in the house, my wife found two lamb chops in the freezer and defrosted them. As she started to cook them, she was still searching for more food for dinner and found some baloney and stale white bread. The smell of the lamb chops cooking

Sophie supervising the preparation of a lamb roast

filled the house with a wonderful aroma, and Sophie sat in the kitchen with her nose in the air, sniffing intently. That night,

Sophie ate the lamb chops for dinner, while my wife and I ate baloney on white toast!

Lamb became one of Sophie's favorite foods. Above is a photograph of Sophie watching Uncle Jim preparing a special leg of lamb for a family dinner.

As Sophie got older, she was getting a lot of special food and extra care. In Sophie's last two years, Sophie and Pixie would still eat together side by side. Some of the times when she would get something special, Pixie did not. As I watched, Sophie would intentionally drop a few pieces of her special food on the floor for Pixie. I have never seen a dog that would share her food with another dog; it was amazing.

Pixie guarding Sophie from everyone while Sophie is sleeping

My original thought was to have Sophie help train Rosebud for therapy work. It was my mistake, as the age difference between the two was too great (age twelve versus puppy). The first six months it turned into a daily exercise of keeping an active puppy away from an older dog. Sophie would not put the puppy in her place, and it became the job of Pixie, the six-pound papillon, to be the protector of Sophie for the last year of her life. If Sophie was sleeping, Pixie would prevent Rosebud from getting close enough to wake Sophie, even nipping at her if necessary.

Sophie and Rosebud eventually accommodated each other. Gentle Sophie was the leader of the pack; but as she aged, she allowed Pixie to be the boss, just as Sophie had allowed Lizzy to be boss when she came into our home. Pixie, a six-pound papillon, became the alpha over two large collies, and remains alpha today.

Pixie, Sophie, and Rosebud

CHAPTER 10

Discovering Alternative Medicine

When is the "right" time to introduce alternative medicine—puppyhood or old age? Usually pet owners have the "don't fix it unless it's broke" attitude. That is what I did with Sophie until the latter part of 2012. Maybe it wasn't the right choice and maybe she should have been treated earlier in her life, but that is not what happened.

Once Sophie turned eleven, she began to have some physical problems. At a very young age, she had fallen off a groomer's table from a height of three to four feet at a large pet store. She was not properly secured with a leash or guard during the grooming process, and when she fell off the table, she injured her hip. Although nothing appeared to be broken, and the X-rays were negative, the bruising and trauma were significant. Even though she was at a young age, it took Sophie almost a month to fully recover and get back to her "normal" self. I believe this was one of the two primary causes of her physical difficulties later in life. The other issue was a reaction to a change in flea protection medicine prescribed by a former veterinarian that was dangerous that was exacerbated by Sophie's MDR1 status. MDR1 status refers to a "multidrug" mutant recessive gene in some breeds that causes complications with medications and treatments. Sophie was tested and was determined to be a "double mutant," indicating that both of her parents carried this gene.

As Sophie began to have walking issues, we were not going to do any invasive procedures such as surgery, as the recovery period would be too long and stressful. But Sophie started having issues with tripping and general neurological issues, and we knew we needed to do something. When traditional veterinary medicine couldn't answer what was wrong, or the solution appeared too traumatic, we sought out nontraditional methods. We found a canine acupuncturist who worked on Sophie for a couple of months with some limited success. Although Sophie was better, she still exhibited unsteadiness. With her work at the hospital appearing to be in jeopardy, I decided it was time to step up and expand her treatment. The acupuncturist was almost an hour's drive away, so going more often was difficult, and the decision was made to try a different type of alternative treatment.

It was then that we found Dr. Erin O'Connor of Vitality Chiropractic Clinic in Aurora, Illinois, only fifteen minutes from home. She treated pets in coordination with a vet for orthopedic issues. Dr. O'Connor's picture is on the back cover of this book. It is one of my favorite pictures. I asked Dr. O'Connor to review her notes over the two years plus that she treated Sophie, and I have summarized her comments. They follow:

Part 1
Alternative Medicine Help

Dr. Erin O'Connor:

Sophie came to my clinic in March 2013. She displayed neurological issues such as an ataxic (wobbly) gait, instability, weak in her rear, and stumbling in her front end since January 2012. Her family had tried treatment for this elsewhere, as well as some supplements and medication. In addition to the neurological issues, more of a critical issue, she had started limping the day before as well as panting excessively.

Dr. Vivian Grant and Dr. Erin O'Connor

I observed Sophie walking through the waiting room to the adjusting room in my office. She was having a difficult time and couldn't walk very well. Her gait was very stiff, movement was limited, there was a very noticeable head bob with each step taken, sometimes stumbling when attempting to move a front limb, and her rear right limb especially looked stiff. Mentally, she looked a bit depressed and seemed to have lost the spark in her eyes. She was up in age for a collie, coming to see me at eleven-and-a-half years old. Chiropractic care usually is a wonderful treatment for senior pets to help improve mobility and function, decrease any discomfort, increase energy, and extend quality of life. As I watched Sophie, I knew it would take some time to work on her issues, and hoped that would be the case with her as well.

It was time for Sophie's first adjustment with me. Before beginning, I always check how familiar each of my clients is with chiropractic care and explain what I am going to do so they understand everything. As I started checking her rear legs, Sophie, a typically friendly dog, gave us a nose scrunch and vocalized that she was not very happy with what was happening. Sophie's owner, surprised, said, "Whoa!" Sophie was in pain and what she did was a normal behavior in response to that. It is not indicative of typical personality. A person would simply tell us. Dogs don't have that ability. However, they can still communicate things such as this quite well! The good thing was, I use two different chiropractic adjustment methods, manual adjustments performed by hand and Activator Method carried out with a small instrument. Practiced proficiently by a qualified animal chiropractor, both methods have the same effectiveness, so I use *whichever I feel is best suited for the patient. With either method, most animals enjoy getting adjusted, because they quickly learn that it makes them feel better, therefore becoming a positive experience. If they have many problem areas, they are very sensitive, or not fond of someone in their personal bubble, The Activator Method tends to be the best method for them.*

Sophie responded well to her first adjustment. She was no longer limping or panting excessively, but was still having some difficulty walking and was tripping. She showed a significant improvement, especially for a dog Sophie's age and having multiple issues, so we continued.

Ten days later, after her second adjustment, she displayed a square sit in the room. Sophie's owners were impressed and said that they hadn't seen her sit like that for a while. With each of the following adjustments, Sophie, however large or small, showed a positive change. After her fourth adjustment, slightly over two months from starting care with me, Sophie's owners reported she seemed to have more energy and was in a happier mood.

What an amazing transformation for Sophie in a relatively short period of time! She now enjoyed her walks again. We had found an important key in helping her transition to her senior years from an old, unstable dog to a happier, more mobile member of the family. After several months of seeing Dr. O'Connor, the acupuncturist we had been taking Sophie to took a medical leave from her practice, and we continued on with just chiropractic care. When we realized that although the care from Dr. O'Connor helped tremendously, Sophie still needed more care. That is when Dr. O'Connor recommended we see Dr. Vivian Grant from Autumn Green Animal Hospital in Geneva. I asked Dr. Grant to review her notes of eighteen months of treating Sophie.

Dr. Vivian Grant:

Sophie first came into my life October 12, 2013. Bernie and Ted brought her in for an acupuncture treatment. She was a beautiful, intelligent collie who recently had become nervous, was panting a lot, and had lost seven pounds of body weight after they had brought a new puppy, named Rosebud, home. Ted and Bernie informed me of her MDR1 mutation, which both of her parents had. This genetic mutation meant she was sensitive to certain medications. Bloodwork done six months earlier showed an elevated ALP (alkaline phosphatase) of 293 U/L. This enzyme most commonly goes high with liver inflammation, bone disease, intestinal issues. I do a lot of nutritional counseling in my practice, as I have learned from my patients, their owners, and my children with food allergies how food plays such an important role in everyone's health. The majority of disease I see is due to problems with nutrition and toxic chemicals my patients are exposed to. I felt Sophie's intestinal problems were a result of her diet, stress/cortisone production, or endocrine disorders. Therefore, I recommended that we change her diet completely to wheat-free/gluten-free food, treats, and anything else fed to her. Farm-raised fish have become my second most common allergen after wheat. Thus, I recommend fish-free food and treats as well.

I also recommended Sophie be fed wheat-free/gluten-free/fish-free food, treats, and table food. I told the Slupiks that organic vegetables and fruits were fine. Bernie started feeding turkey, chicken, sweet potato, eggs, bone marrow soup, carrots, and a probiotic. Two different supplements from Standard Process were added into her meals. By eating healthy organs, the building blocks for Sophie's damaged organs were provided to allow her body to heal.

During my first acupuncture session, I examined Sophie's tongue, pulse, and temperament. Using traditional Chinese Veterinary Medicine, a Spleen Qi Deficiency and a Heart Yin Deficiency were diagnosed. The Spleen Qi Deficiency resulted in diarrhea and muscle loss. Her anxiety was due to an imbalance of her heart meridian. Therefore, acupuncture points were chosen to address both of those issues. Acupuncture helps the body heal

Sophie taking a nap during acupuncture

itself. At first Sophie was a little nervous and did not like any points on her front legs below the elbows. After a couple of sessions her diarrhea improved, she gained a little weight, and she would calm down for a few days post treatment. During the future acupuncture treatments she would lie down and relax after the needles were placed.

In the first couple of sessions Sophie was put into an exam room that contained children's play area and toy bin. In the bin was a Barbie doll with multi-colored hair that Sophie took out and kept with her during her treatment. It was a doll my daughter had when she was younger. There was something about this doll that Sophie loved. She would find it every time that particular exam room was used. Unfortunately, one day the doll could not be found. No one at the animal hospital had seen it or knew where it had gone. Sophie would look for that doll every time she was placed in that room. We felt bad so we tried not to put her in that room after that; however, she always looked for that doll if we had to use that room.

After six acupuncture sessions and Sophie's diet being changed, bloodwork was repeated on November 16, 2013. Her ALP had become normal at 115U/L. The normal range for our lab is 20-150U/L. Several days' later blood was taken in order to check her thyroid levels, which turned out to be normal.

What an amazing difference we noticed in Sophie with simple changes of diet and alternative medicine treatments of chiropractic, acupuncture, and laser treatments. The battle that we had been fighting eased, her blood tests improved significantly, and she seemed happier. Sophie began to eat and enjoy her meals more almost immediately. I would not have believed this if I had not seen it with my own eyes.

Part 2
The Unknown of the MDR-1 Mutation and How It Affected Sophie

Dr. Erin O'Connor:

Sophie had some struggles with instability, tripping with her front legs, and weakness in her rear. Although chiropractic helped to improve these areas, they seemed to happen on a regular basis. I think it is important to digress a moment to explain that some of Sophie's neurological issues may have been from receiving heartworm medication and flea protection treatments. There is a gene called MDR-1, which stands for multi-drug resistance. The highest frequency of dog breeds affected by this gene is in herding breeds, with about one-third of collie breeds being homozygous recessive (having two copies of the mutated allele making up the MDR-1 gene from parents) and close to half being heterozygous (carriers). Sophie was homozygous, having two copies of the mutated allele, making her highly vulnerable to adverse reactions to particular medications, such as certain heartworm preventatives and flea protection. The area of the nervous system that the drug affects in parasites is usually behind a normal functioning "barrier" in the dog that the medication can't reach. This isn't the case with being homozygous recessive for MDR-1, which can lead to deficits from neurologic toxicity if the medications they are sensitive to are administered. Unfortunately, that was the case with Sophie. It was still nice to observe that even though she probably had some irreversible neurological damage from that, these areas still could receive some benefit from chiropractic care.

Part 3
Ongoing Treatments and Refinement of Sophie's Care

Dr. O'Connor and Dr. Grant bonded with Sophie. They worked in coordination with each other and reviewed each other's notes to customize Sophie's treatment plan. During her treatments, I would often tell them some of the amazing stories of Sophie, and knowing her personality helped with the plan. They wanted to keep Sophie enjoying life almost as much as I did. Sophie's gait continued to improve dramatically. She was walking better at age twelve than at age eleven.

Dr. Vivian Grant:

In February 2014, Bernie Slupik had a session with Asia Voight, an animal communicator I had taken a class from. According to Asia, many things were discussed; however, she found out that the right side of Sophie's face/jaw hurt her. I translated that to be TMJ (temporomandibular joint) disease, which was causing pain and making it difficult for her to eat. On February 10, 2014, I included local acupuncture points on her that would help her jaw pain, as well as did a therapeutic laser treatment on her. The therapeutic laser has a wavelength of light that stimulates macrophages to clean up damaged tissue and decrease inflammation. Dr. O'Connor also started adjusting her TMJ. All three modalities seemed to help her quite a bit. We were all very pleased with the information Asia Voight was able to provide.

Dr. Erin O'Connor:

One variable in Sophie's case that had been checked and adjusted for a couple of short periods in her care was her left TMJ (temporomandibular joint). This finding showed up in a third phase. Just before her TMJ was causing trouble again, Sophie had an appointment with an animal communicator and communicated that her TMJ was in pain. Although this wasn't a central area that was consistently adjusted prior, it became so at her next and future appointments with me. Her owners thought it was interesting that the animal communication correlated with the chiropractic findings at our visit and improved her ability to eat her food, which was imperative for Sophie, considering her underweight state.

Sophie grew to enjoy coming in for her adjustments which were about every two weeks, and she clearly had a set routine. For instance, I had a basket of dog Frisbees in my waiting room and it was necessary for her to check the basket each time. When the basket was gone, she searched for it at several visits following. She would then continue to the treatment room and walk over for a greeting and some pets from me. Next, it was time to discuss how Sophie has been doing and begin her treatment. I started on her rear legs and worked my way up through her back, ribs, front legs, neck, and head. She had some eccentricities during her treatment. After having anything she needed to be adjusted in her rear, I would perform a chiropractic technique that allows the deep musculature in the rear and back to relax. It's a very minimal stimulus of light pressure applied to a specific area that causes maximal relaxation and reduction of muscle strain. As soon as I would press my thumb on one of these areas, she would sit down on my lap with bright eyes, relaxed, and a smile. That had to be one her favorite parts of her visit.

On the other hand, her least favorite part of her visit was her front legs being touched. She had been putting extra weight on her front legs after her rear became weak. She knew when it was time for that part and would pull her front feet away before I even touched them. Sophie's family started bringing a towel to cover her head; this helped her relax, and sometimes I think she started dozing off under there while I worked on her legs, as it looked like she just woke up when we would take the towel off.

Another favorite of hers, treats! She never missed a piece of bacon jerky treat that her family brought to her visits, as well as her freeze-dried lamb treat that she'd beeline for after standing up from her adjustment and giving a good shake-off.

The deep-muscle relaxation technique that Dr. O'Connor describes in this previous section must have made Sophie's muscles feel amazing. The back cover of this book shows this treatment and Sophie's obvious enjoyment of it.

Part 4
Sophie's Weight Issues

Dr. Erin O'Connor:

Even though Sophie had a voracious appetite, eating more food than a typical dog her size, she was underweight and had trouble gaining and keeping the weight she had. Lack of weight contributed to the lack of stability, strength, and muscular support for her body, hence her inability to hold her adjustments as long as a dog at their ideal weight and with quality muscular support.

Dr. Vivian Grant:

Sophie continued to lose weight, so Bernie would cook for her on a regular basis in an effort to have her gain weight. In September 2014 I prescribed minerals to help replace any deficiencies, and Bernie started Sophie back on digestive enzymes in an effort to help her absorb nutrients of the food she was eating. Also, at this time Bernie found a new organic baby food that Sophie loved to eat. We were hopeful that she would start to gain weight.

Every time Sophie would gain a few pounds between visits, she would lose it by the next visit. We were never able to solve the mystery of her losing weight. For whatever reason, her body could not absorb her calories.

CHAPTER 11

The Christmas Miracle

We were quite surprised and very grateful that Sophie survived to celebrate her thirteenth birthday in September 2014, based on her burgeoning health issues. Most collies live somewhere between the age of twelve and fourteen, and Sophie had the decks stacked against her with her double-mutant MDR1 status. We knew her time was limited, but she continued to do therapy work at the hospital until February because *she* wanted to. Sophie would still show her excitement whenever she was visiting at the hospital as her adrenalin would start flowing.

Christmas in 2014 was a short workweek. December 22 was Monday, Christmas Eve was on a Wednesday, and Thursday was the Christmas Day holiday. Bernie and I were at the office on Monday, about to start the office Christmas party, when we received a very distressing call from our pet walker. Sophie had apparently slipped and fallen in the laundry room, and was unable to stand or get up.

Sophie liked the cool tile of the laundry room. In her later years, due to her age and orthopedic issues, Sophie had some difficulty walking on wood floors and tile. Unfortunately, our house on the first floor had mostly wood floors. We put down area rugs and runners throughout the house to make her walking and daily life easier. She could get up and down and walk on a carpet fairly easily. The only place we did not have a rug was a 3' x 3' section in the laundry room. The tile was usually cool, and Sophie found that comforting. That, unfortunately, was the place she picked to stand, turn around and fall that day.

We rushed home to see Sophie completely splayed in the corner by the laundry room door. Her front feet were straight out and her back legs were out to each side of her. She was panting, obviously dehydrated and in distress. The vet later told us she was also in shock from repeatedly trying to get up out of the corner on her own, which probably went on for a period of several hours. Her energy level was spent, and the gleam in her eyes was gone. When we tried to stand her, Sophie could not stand or bear her weight without support. We immediately took her to the vet.

We carried her to the van and put her on a blanket in the back. My wife sat in the back with her during the trip. Of course traffic was horrible. It was raining, and it took what seemed forever to get to the vet. That day (a Monday) both Dr. Grant and Dr. O'Connor were at the clinic at the same time. Dr. O'Connor had her own office, but this day she happened to be at Dr. Grant's facility. Coincidence? I think not.

We had to carry Sophie into the office. Dr. Grant's staff knew her well and were upset to see Sophie in such distress and being carried in. We immediately saw Dr. Grant and asked her what she thought the available options were. I did not think we would be given any favorable options that day. We knew there couldn't be much hope, and we didn't want to extend Sophie's life if there was no chance for recovery.

Based on Dr. Grant's extensive knowledge of the dog, including Sophie's will to live and survive, she agreed to try a couple treatments for a few days to see if it improved things. We would do subcutaneous fluids for Sophie's dehydration and some acupuncture points and laser treatment to sooth the muscles that were in spasm. Nothing appeared to be broken, nor was there any sign of internal bleeding. Dr. Grant started the acupuncture and went to the next room to see a German shepherd who was also in a difficult situation. The German shepherd was there with internal bleeding, and the owners were trying to decide whether to put the dog down. So here we were in the adjacent room, overhearing parts of the conversation about the German shepherd's possible fate, hearing the owners crying, and knowing that the end result could be the same for Sophie as well. The couple with the German shepherd decided to try a couple things that day and to come back later in the week to see Dr. Grant. After the fact, we found out that the couple had been back on Wednesday (Christmas Eve) and had to put the German shepherd down.

After the laser treatments and fluids, Sophie saw Dr. O'Connor. She did chiropractic adjustments to help ease the pain and stop the pulsating muscles. At the end of the treatment, Sophie was able to slightly stand with support, but we still knew the chances of recovery were remote. We took her home and stopped at a pet store to purchase a harness. The treatment was now to let her rest for two or three days and see whether there was improvement. If there was improvement, we would continue with the treatment; if there was no improvement by Wednesday (Christmas Eve), Sophie would be put down.

She struggled to eat and drink the remainder of Monday, and we finally got her to drink some water and urinate after almost a 24-hour period on Tuesday morning. We decided, based on an ever-so-slight improvement, to take her for another chiropractic treatment on Tuesday night. Dr. O'Connor, always a wonderful and caring doctor, altered her schedule for us and was able to spend quite a bit of time with Sophie at the end of the day. Dr. O'Connor indicated the muscles had stopped the spasm, but it was still too soon to tell what and how much the recovery would be. We went to sleep Tuesday night afraid to wake up to what would happen on Wednesday morning.

What happened next cannot be explained. My wife came down in the morning to check on Sophie, who was sleeping in the laundry room for the night. That was her favorite place to sleep, as it was the coolest room in the house. My wife was sitting in the family room on the couch where she could see Sophie in the laundry room while looking at her pictures on her phone. Out of nowhere and on her own, Sophie got up and started walking into the family room. My wife was so astonished she turned on the video camera on her cell phone and recorded this moment, which we will treasure forever.

Sophie walked into the family room at her normal pace, looked around, checked in her secret spot under the window seat cushion for cookies she sometimes hid, and then came toward us. It was as if nothing had happened two days prior. She got up and the look in her eyes and the smile said, "I'm still here and I'm going to be okay; thanks for taking care of me."

We still had our follow-up appointment with Dr. Grant on Christmas Eve morning, which we were going to keep. The staff saw Sophie come into the reception area under her own power

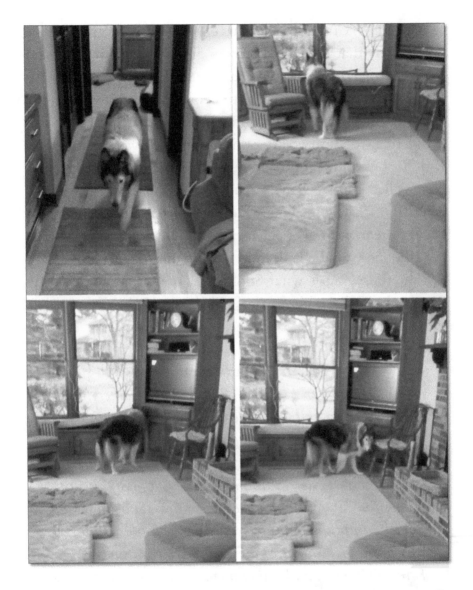

and began to cheer and cry. No one ever expected her to walk again, let alone to walk almost normally two days later. When Dr. Grant walked into the examination room and saw Sophie, she also began to cry. She had witnessed the unbelievable will of Sophie to continue.

I asked Dr. Grant, "What chance would you have given Sophie on Monday that she would recover and walk again?" She said that she would have put that chance at less than 10 percent. We showed Dr. Grant the video we took of Sophie getting up on her own that morning, and Dr. Grant became misty again. For a period of a week or two after this incident, we were very careful with Sophie coming into and out of rooms, going outside, and limiting her access to stairs. Sophie recovered back to her strength before the accident in about a month, and we were given the gift of six more months of Sophie being with us. Sophie remembered her fall, and would not sleep in the laundry room again.

The following is what Sophie's two alternative medicine doctors had to say about our "Christmas Miracle" and her subsequent care:

Dr. Vivian Grant:

On December 22, 2014, Sophie's pet walker found her splayed out and unable to walk. On examination her gums were pale and her muscles in her front legs were having spasms. Bloodwork was done which showed a stress response, dehydration, and low potassium. Low potassium can result in muscle weakness. Subcutaneous fluids with potassium added were given, potassium gel was prescribed, a chiropractic adjustment done by Dr. Erin O'Connor, and a therapeutic laser treatment was done. We theorized that Sophie had slipped and hurt her right hip and left wrist. We were all very concerned as to whether she would be able to recover or were we getting close to the end. Sophie went home. Bernie called the following day to let us know that Sophie had finally urinated 24 hours later and she was able to stand. She was still very wobbly and unsteady on her feet, but she walked. Two days later we repeated the laser treatment and she received an acupuncture treatment. Her color was better and she seemed stronger. Her will to live was much stronger than most collies I have treated in the past. Ted was not willing to lose her yet.

Dr. Erin O'Connor:

December 22, 2014, was a significant day for Sophie and her family. On that date Sophie had fallen while her family was at work and was found by her pet walker lying splayed on the floor. It seemed like she had been struggling in that position for some time. After being found, she could not stand or walk. At her age, thirteen years old, falling and struggling took a toll on her body. Her family didn't think she would make it. Her vet also didn't think she would recover. However, her family decided to give her a chance to make a recovery. She was brought to me for an adjustment, and at that adjustment she laid on the floor the entire visit. She was very weak and tired. Her muscles felt beyond overworked. I adjusted her and did a lot of soft tissue work at that visit as well, to try and speed up the healing process as much as I could for a senior dog in her situation. She came in for another adjustment the next evening. Despite still not being back to herself, she seemed to feel better and also had gained a little strength. There was hope. I did nearly the same adjustment as I did on her last visit and she went home. The next day, December 24, 2014, she stood up and walked around as if nothing had happened. Her family refers to this date as "the Christmas Miracle."

Continued Care with a Step-Up in Frequency

Dr. Erin O'Connor:

We were able to get back to our usual care schedule, which since the spring of 2015 was once a week. Sophie wasn't holding her adjustments as long as she used

Dr. O'Connor and Sophie, May 2015

to, needing more frequent adjustments as she grew older. This led to Tuesday nights with Sophie. Every Tuesday since the spring I would go through my day starting at 8:00 a.m. seeing patients. The last patient of the day at 7:45 p.m. was Sophie. With Sophie and her routine and quirks, this seemed to be a good time slot for her.

At one of these visits, in late May 2015, we were able to capture Sophie's favorite part of her visit on camera. Sophie displayed bright eyes and a big grin on her face while sitting on my lap as I held a light pressure point to relieve deep muscle tension. I posted this on my clinic's Facebook page with the caption, "At 14 years old, Sophie has her ways. If she wants to sit on Dr.

O'Connor's lap during part of her chiropractic adjustment, that's A-OK!" Many people connected with Sophie's picture if they had a soft spot for senior dogs, enjoyed her smile, thought she was beautiful, or merely were surprised some-thing like chiropractic existed for pets. A few other animal chiropractors shared the picture as well, since they, like me, understand how much chiropractic can help a senior pet. Sophie's picture received over 250 likes and comments in only a day or so.

Christmas, 2014

Dr. Vivian Grant:

In January 2015 we continued treating Sophie with acupuncture, subcutaneous fluids, laser treatment, and pain meds every two weeks. She had regained her strength and was doing better. Over the next several months Sophie lost muscle mass. Her anxiety with Rosebud greatly decreased and she loved her home-cooked meals. In February, she went on medical leave

Christmas morning breakfast (bacon)

from being a therapy dog at Edward's Hospital. I told Bernie that Sophie was too weak to vaccinate, which was required for her to keep going as a therapy dog. Sophie's will to live persisted and Ted was not ready for her to go. Bernie and I both knew until Ted gave her permission to go, she would stay around. I would see her almost every two weeks for acupuncture, subcutaneous fluids, and laser treatments as needed.

CHAPTER 12

The Last Six Months

After Sophie's recovery and Christmas Eve, I knew there wouldn't be a whole lot of quality time left. At her age, it took her about a month to regain her strength and stamina and be able to go on short walks again. Once she did recover, she wanted to do the things she always did, but could not do them in as great a quantity.

Sophie watching football with friend, Larry

Sophie had many visitors in December, January, and February 2015 when our friends and family heard of her plight. It was almost like everyone was coming by to say how happy they were that she was still here, and at the same time starting to say goodbye, as nothing could last forever. Over the next six months, at least twenty friends and family came by the house specifically to see Sophie. Although they were very happy to see her, I realized that they were all quietly saying goodbye. Every day from December 24 through June 17 was a gift.

She still went to the hospital to visit patients. Rather than being able to work two and a half hours, she was able to work about one and a half hours. We could still see the look in Sophie's eyes and the adrenaline start flowing when she was prepared to go to the hospital as always. She *knew* we were going when I got out my blue coat and she got her name tag and special collar put on. The last six months at the hospital had become known as our farewell tour. We informed all the nurses and patients who knew us that Sophie was going to retire very soon. In addition to working at the hospital, she continued to visit friends and patients at a local nursing home up until May. Although there were a few difficult days, there was much more good than bad.

Sophie was a creature of habit, and the older she got, the more stubborn she became about her habits. My wife was usually home about an hour before me. Every day, Sophie waited for me to come home from work, either inside in the front family room window or outside in the front yard. She seemed to have a sense that it was time for me to be home. Even when my wife called her to come back into the house, she refused. Some days the wait was longer than other days, but it didn't matter to her. She would stay on her post until I got home.

We still did the things in the spring of her last year that we did every year, such as going to the lake in April. Although we went to the lake for a couple hours, we didn't take the hour-long walk around it, but only walked for about half the time. Sophie still seemed to thoroughly enjoy it as she looked all around her, taking everything in. Sophie also looked forward to taking boat rides on a pontoon boat. You could tell it was one of her favorite activities as she stood perfectly with her head in the wind and the breeze blowing through her face and her mane. She was almost always smiling when she was doing this. Other than eating, going on the boat was Sophie's favorite activity.

Sophie and her nurse fans on her last day of work

Once we got into January with her recovery, Sophie started to become unsettled at night and didn't sleep as well. She would either be quite restless, probably because of some arthritic pain, or she would be

Waiting for me to come home from work

thirsty and need a drink of water, or she would just get up needing to go to the bathroom. As Sophie slept in our bedroom on
her bed, my wife and I would basically lie there, stare, and watch
her all night to make sure everything was okay. Although we
thought this was a good idea, it resulted in neither of us getting
much sleep most nights. I came up with a solution that surpris-
ingly worked very well.

Last boat ride on a chilly day in May

I took an inflatable mattress and laid it next to Sophie, and
decided to spend most of the night on the floor next to her. If she
woke up, I would wake up and be able to handle the situation.
If she didn't wake up, both of us got a pretty good night's sleep.
This went on for the remaining period of her life. It sounds like

it was hard, but it really was easy. Sophie felt confident that if she needed anything when I was lying next to her, all she would have to do is get up and it would be handled. As a matter of fact, she liked my mattress so much, many nights she would push me off the mattress during the night onto the floor and put her head on my pillow. There was almost a grin on her face in the morning, waking up and knowing she got the better of the sleeping arrangement.

Sophie continued to lose weight, and it was harder for her to eat. One of the foods we started to give her as a supplement was organic baby food in a pouch twice a day. It seemed to work well and she enjoyed it very much. It provided protein and vegetables in a soft form which was very easy for her to chew and digest. Sophie was generally in control of her bowel movements up until the very end as well. In order to make sure of this, we had to change her routine. We needed more time in the morning to feed her and leave for the office, so we started to get up early at 5:30 a.m.

Our dog walker, Dolores, was a wonderful person who helped as well. Rather than letting Sophie and the other dogs out at noon, she would come by at 10:30, take Sophie out, bring her back in, and come back at about 1:00 or 1:30. This limited the accidents Sophie could have. She did have one or two in her later years.

We were going for biweekly acupuncture and chiropractic treatments, and she seemed to be doing great. The vet and chiropractor seemed to think she was doing better and would probably be around awhile. In my heart and from previous experience, I knew the end was going to come soon. Her last two months were mostly with adrenaline flowing, and you would not know she was almost a fourteen-year-old dog. Although she could get up easily from a sitting position, it was sometimes difficult and becoming painful for her to sit and lie down. We would need to help her on occasion; and although the acupuncture helped some, it was clear pain was becoming an issue.

One Sunday in June, Sophie and I were sitting together in the family room. She was lying next to me and I was sitting on the floor. I looked at her, began to stroke her, and I began to cry. I knew she had gotten to a point where she wanted to go, and she was sticking around because of me. "It's okay to say goodbye now, Sophie," I told her. "I understand, I know it's time. Thank you for being the best friend I ever had." I'll never forget the way Sophie looked at me at that moment. I knew she understood.

The final goodbye came on Wednesday.

Following are comments from Sophie's two alternative medicine doctors about that last Wednesday . . .

June 17, 2015

Dr Vivian Grant:

Sophie's treatment continued until June 17, 2015. She came in because she had trouble walking. Upon entering the clinic, she could not stand. Her back legs were crossing. Sophie used the wall in the exam room to stand. On palpation her intestines felt thickened. A CBC/Comprehensive Diagnostic panel was run, which showed dehydration and slightly low potassium. Everything else was normal. She had lost so much weight, looked like she was ready to leave this world, and Ted was finally ready to let her go. I was informed that he had given her permission "to go" a few days before. On June 17, 2015, I euthanized Sophie. I knew it was a gift I could give to her to help her move on to the spiritual world.

Bernie and Ted gave me permission to do a necropsy and send off tissues to try to find out more details on what caused her problems. Nothing obvious stood out except that her heart was small and undersized on necropsy. I sent off samples of her liver, kidney, spleen, intestines (jejunum), lungs, heart, and right hip. No cancer was found. She had arthritis of her right hip, congested intestines, and septic pneumonia thought to be due to aspiration (inhaled food). The villi of the intestines were normal and there was nothing to indicate poor absorption of food. Bacteria were found in her lungs, so pneumonia was technically what weakened her at the very end.

Sophie showed me how a strong will to live can overcome many obstacles. Her bond with Ted and Bernie was special. Ted and Bernie's love for Sophie kept her going. Sophie's love for them gave them the impetus to take care of her and treat her the best they knew how. I will always remember how she loved her acupuncture sessions and would go to sleep while the needles would energize her. She ended up receiving a total of thirty-nine acupuncture treatments over two years. During these sessions, I enjoyed spending time with the Slupiks conversing about Sophie and listening to stories about her. She was a special dog whose physical presence will be missed.

Dr. Erin O'Connor:

I received a text from Sophie's owner explaining that she wanted to let me know that Sophie passed away that afternoon, as well as saying, "We'd like to thank you for all you have done over the last two years for her. You certainly made a huge difference in her quality of life. We miss her terribly." I responded with my sympathies for Sophie and on how she truly did have a quality life until the very end, remarking that she happily took her treat the night before. I'd like to close the story of my time with Sophie with the last three text messages of that conversation:

"Thanks for all your effort and caring for Sophie. I'm convinced you kept her going for us for a long time. We appreciate it!"

"You're welcome. My Tuesday night won't be the same without Miss Sophie."

"Ours won't be the same either."

Afterword

The definition of the word coincidence is: *"a remarkable concurrence of events or circumstance without apparent causal connection."* There were many "coincidences" in Sophie's life. Coincidences with the people she met, the people she helped with her therapy work, and, of course, coincidences within our own family. In this book, I have told you a few of the stories of Sophie's impact on the people she met. When a family loses a loved and valued family pet, the family experiences sadness and loss for a time. Eventually, that sadness is replaced by fond memories.

Our family has experienced this sadness and resulting fond memories multiple times prior to being fortunate enough to share our lives with Sophie. She, however, was different than most pets. The impact she had on so many people in the same way was not planned by me or Sophie. Did these events happen by accident, chance, serendipity, providence, happenstance, or fate? A coincidence? I think not.

The outpouring after Sophie's passing was unbelievable. Hundreds of friends, family members, or clients who knew Sophie all expressed sympathy. They thought she would go on forever.

Her will to live and to continue making people feel better cannot be expressed in words.

There is no doubt that the grief I felt with Sophie's passing was intense. Our friends and family were deeply moved by her and felt the loss sincerely. In the immediateness of her passing, sympathies from family and friends were comforting. However, when day-to-day life began again, the loss that I felt was almost unbearable. I'm sure that people who never experienced such a bond thought perhaps the loss affected me too much.

It was obvious by their actions that Sophie's housemates, Pixie and Rosebud, grieved over the loss of their friend as well. Their reactions sometimes made it even more difficult to recover from Sophie being gone. Sophie was spoiled during her senior years and had multiple beds throughout the house. After she passed, we removed all the beds except the one in our room. We left the bed in our bedroom where Sophie slept every night for quite some time. Neither dog would step foot on it, even after it was laundered. It was *Sophie's* bed, meant for her, and they both knew it. Even though Sophie was no longer here, they respected her place in the house.

After a period of time, we finally took it away and let Rosebud come up and sleep in our room with Pixie. To this day, neither Pixie nor Rosebud will sleep in the same place that Sophie slept for all those years. Rosebud's bed had to be moved to the opposite side of the room and Sophie's place remains sadly empty. I think that they still occasionally look for Sophie. I know I still do.

But life goes on and when acceptance finally came, it was time to decide whether I should continue grieving and living in the past, or find some way to resume life, honor my friend, and make sure that her legacy carried on. I chose the latter.

First, I concentrated on getting Pixie and Rosebud qualified as therapy dogs so they could visit the sick and elderly. Pixie passed with flying colors, no doubt from her years of watching Sophie. While she does not have the intuition and sensitivity that Sophie had, I am sure that the people she visits find comfort in her. Rosebud, while taking a bit longer to pass the tests, now regularly visits nursing homes, and the residents there look forward to seeing her.

After getting Pixie and Rosebud set for therapy work, I still wanted to make sure Sophie's legacy endured. I became a tester/observer for Alliance for Therapy Dogs, Inc., and have successfully tested, observed, and passed about fifty dogs to date. These dogs, along with their owners, will provide comfort and healing to untold numbers of people and continue Sophie's legacy. I intend to continue training and counseling people and their dogs who want to bring healing and joy to the people who need it the most.

CONCLUSION:

Sophie was very loyal and was a great family dog. She had a devotion in her eyes and a certain friendliness. She was much more than a dog based on her ability to express and extract emotions from the people she encountered. She was my best friend, and best friends are forever.

Epilogue

After the death of our dear Chihuahua, Lizzy, my wife and I decided to establish "Lizzy's Fund" in her memory for the wonderful companionship that she afforded us during her sixteen and a half years as part of our family. Lizzy encountered some severe health issues at age nine, and if it weren't for the compassionate alternative medical care that she received, she most likely would have had to be euthanized. Instead, that unconventional care, relatively new at the time, gave Lizzy the opportunity to enjoy seven-plus more years of quality life with our family.

The purpose of Lizzy's Fund is to aid in the all-encompassing care of senior dogs aged seven and older. It provides full veterinary, dental, and grooming care for senior dogs in shelter and rescue environments. It also covers senior dog adoption fees at the shelters or rescues. In addition to the care it provides, Lizzy's Fund is also an educational resource for people who are considering the adoption of a senior dog and for new senior dog owners who realize how much joy and love older pets can bring into their lives.

Established in 2012, Lizzy's Fund has since helped over three hundred senior dogs find comfort and happiness in compassionate homes. It is a 501(c)(3) charitable organization. All of the net proceeds of this book will be placed in Lizzy's Fund to further the message of how much a human's life can be enriched by caring for a senior dog.

Lizzy's Fund has also expanded its horizon to visiting local schools, talking about Animal Assisted Therapy, and the benefits of volunteering at nursing homes. We currently work with local schools and have a number of student volunteers who regularly devote their time. They assist handlers who, along with their senior dogs, make a difference for the nursing home senior residents on most Sunday mornings.

For more information, please visit *www.lizzysfund.org*.

Acknowledgments

BERNIE: My typist, editor, and spouse who cared about Sophie as much as I did

DR. ERIN O'CONNOR: Animal chiropractor who showed love, encouragement and support for Sophie on *every* visit

DR. VIVIAN GRANT: Eastern and Western medicine and holistic veterinarian who sought alternative treatments for Sophie that extended both Sophie's life and quality of life

LAURA T. COFFEY AND MICHAEL WANN: Friends and author of *My Old Dog: Rescued Pets with Remarkable Second Acts* (Laura) for their encouragement and support

DR. PAUL NOTOLLI: Human chiropractor by day and volunteer website designer by night

MIKE FLEEGE: Graphic designer who worked on the pictures in the book

ERLA: Sophie's caring pet walker early on who was part of her life for fourteen years and who also cared for Lizzy

SOPHIE'S CLOSEST HUMAN FRIENDS: Larry and Linda, Pam and Wayne, and Jan

SOPHIE'S CLOSEST COLLIE FRIENDS: Riley, Rosebud, Pixley, and Mavis

ANIMAL ASSISTED THERAPY PARTNERS:
Paul and Molly (golden retriever)
Macki and Little Pretty (long-haired dachshund)
Laurie and Cherry (Scottish terrier)
Laurie and Lilly (West Highland terrier)

DOLORES: Sophie's last pet walker who kindly went above and beyond her call of duty

AUNT WENDY, UNCLE RON, AND PEPPER (the Dog): Friends who knew Sophie and provided loving care for the puppy Rosebud when needed

LIZZY, PIXIE AND ROSEBUD: Sophie's pals

SOPHIE: The best dog ever . . .

About the Author

This book was a first-time literary effort for me. For my entire career, I was buried in the financial world. I counseled people on monetary and fiscal matters. The hours were long and the work was rewarding, I guess; but when Sophie came into my life, my focus began to change. I had been a dog lover all my life and had a dog as a child and several more dogs from the time my children were small. With Sophie, though, I experienced a devotion and special emotional connection. We spent thousands of hours together. My previous dogs were wonderful pets, but Sophie, she was something special, a one-of-a-kind dog. I always taught obedience to my previous dogs so that they were good family members and courteous to people that they met. While training Sophie, I realized that she had not only the desire to please, but she also had a happy demeanor, sensitivity, and a special connection with the people she met that made it obvious that therapy work was perfectly suited for her. Although I still enjoyed my work, I began to look forward to my Friday nights at the hospital with Sophie. My anticipation matched hers, and together we made a great team. I have no doubt that we helped many people who needed either someone to talk to, or just some quiet consolation on an otherwise lonely Friday night.

I began doing Animal Assisted Therapy work in 2002 with Sophie, and continue now with my current dogs, Pixie and Rosebud. I also have been a tester/observer with the Therapy Dog program run through the Alliance of Therapy Dogs (formerly Therapy Dogs, Inc.) since 2012. My goal in writing this book was to help transmit the feelings and emotions that Sophie exuded to all those she met. If I have accomplished some of that, I consider it a success. Sophie's story was an amazing one, and I realize now that I had a great privilege to accompany her along her journey.

Since this book was initially published, I have continued my writing career and have written more than a dozen articles about dogs, primarily about collies. These articles have been published in *ruffDRAFTS*, the quarterly newsletter of the national organization, Dog Writers Association of America, AWCA (American Working Collie Association), and the *Collie Nose Newsletter.* Based on these articles as well as my book, I was honored to receive a press pass for the 2019 AKC Westminster Dog Show in New York, writing several articles about that event. You can view many stories that I have written at either www.lizzysfund. org or www.sophiebestfriendsforever.com.

CPSIA information can be obtained
at www.ICGtesting.com
Printed in the USA
FSHW011700111119
63982FS